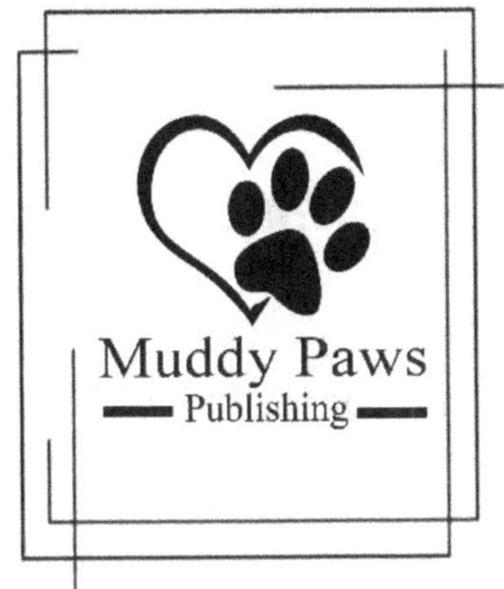

Muddy Paws Publishing is a group of passionate and talented individuals creating fun activity, coloring, and puzzle books for all ages.

We love what we do.

Thank you for choosing Muddy Paws Publishing books

We are always available for support via email at muddypawspublishing@gmail.com

Connect With Us

@muddypawspublishing

  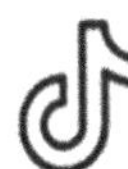 Etsy

This book is dedicated to my brother who served as the inspiration for this book.

He lives his life as an for example for others, is a blessing to everyone he encounters, and attributes all praise and glory to God for the difference he makes in their lives.

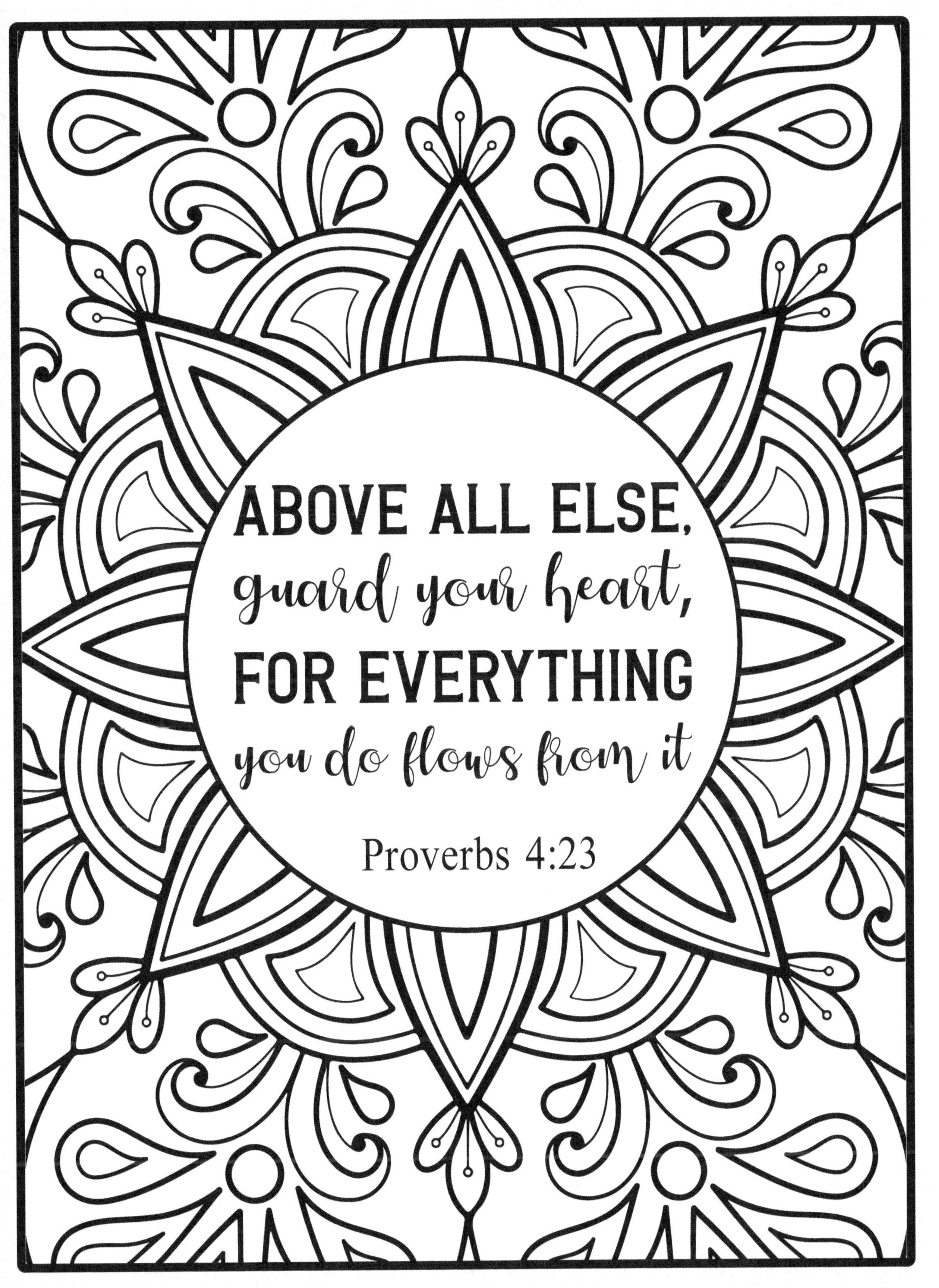

ABOVE ALL ELSE,
guard your heart,
FOR EVERYTHING
you do flows from it
Proverbs 4:23

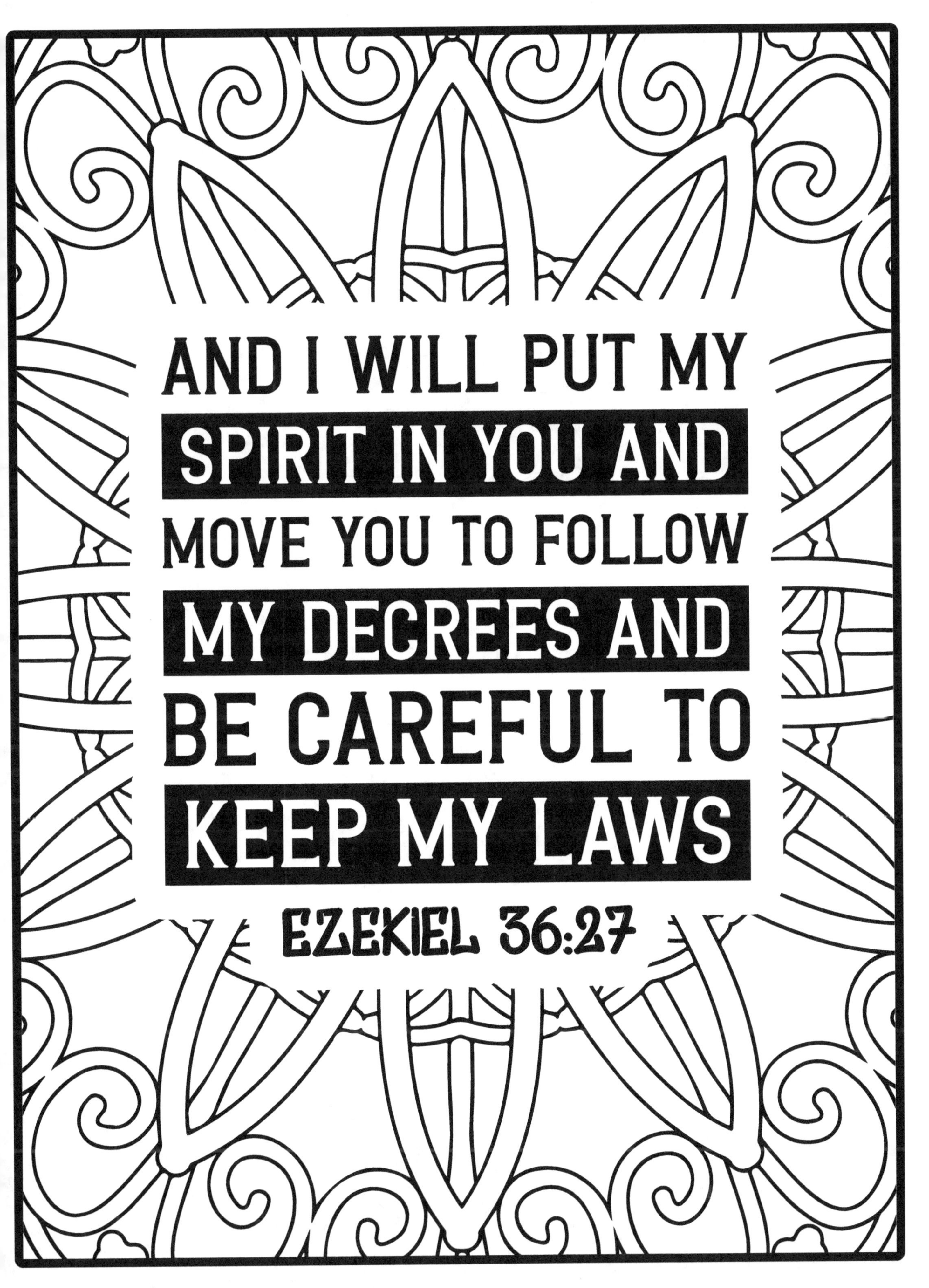

AND I WILL PUT MY SPIRIT IN YOU AND MOVE YOU TO FOLLOW MY DECREES AND BE CAREFUL TO KEEP MY LAWS
EZEKIEL 36:27

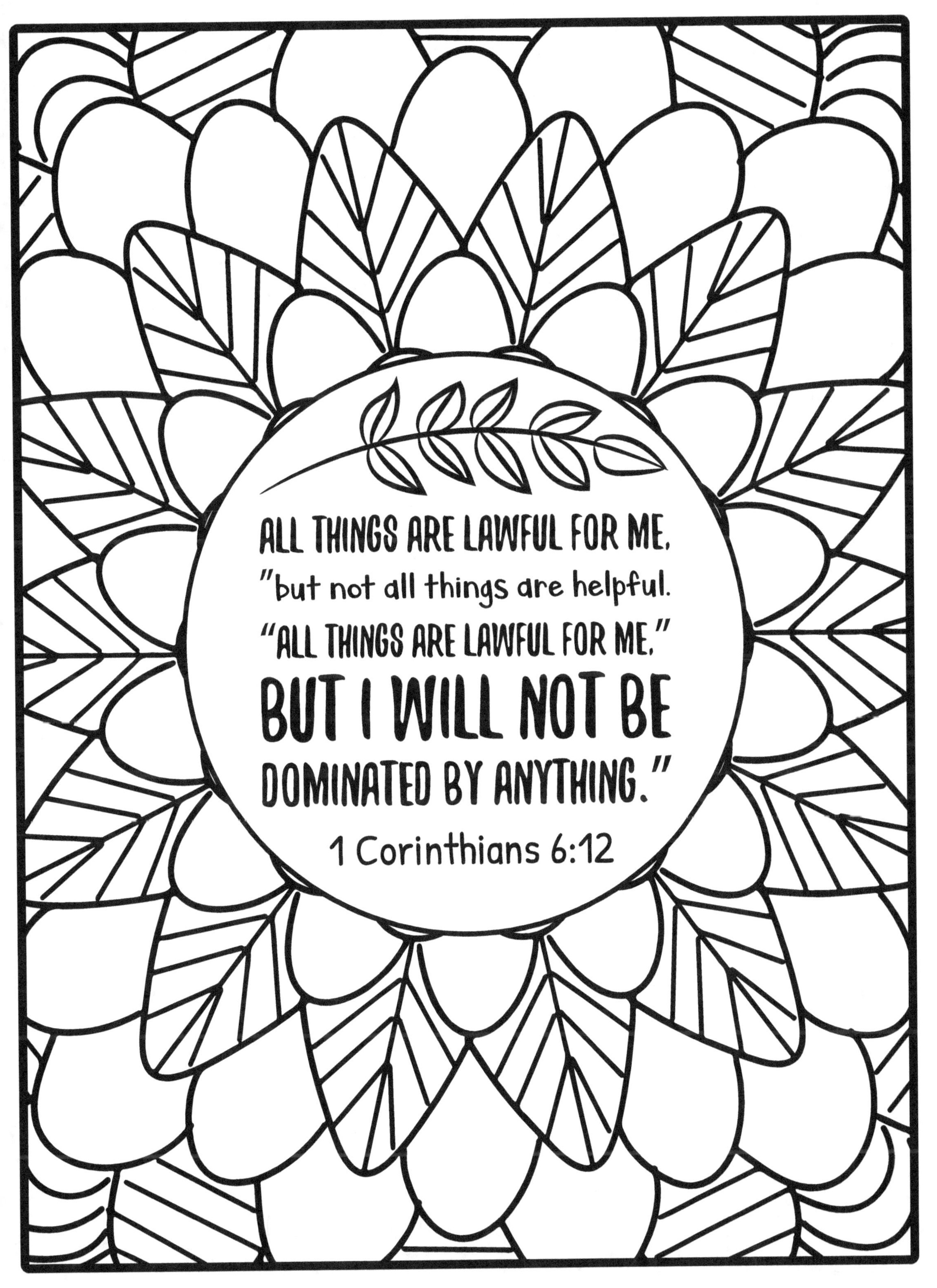

ALL THINGS ARE LAWFUL FOR ME,
"but not all things are helpful.
"ALL THINGS ARE LAWFUL FOR ME,"
BUT I WILL NOT BE
DOMINATED BY ANYTHING."
1 Corinthians 6:12

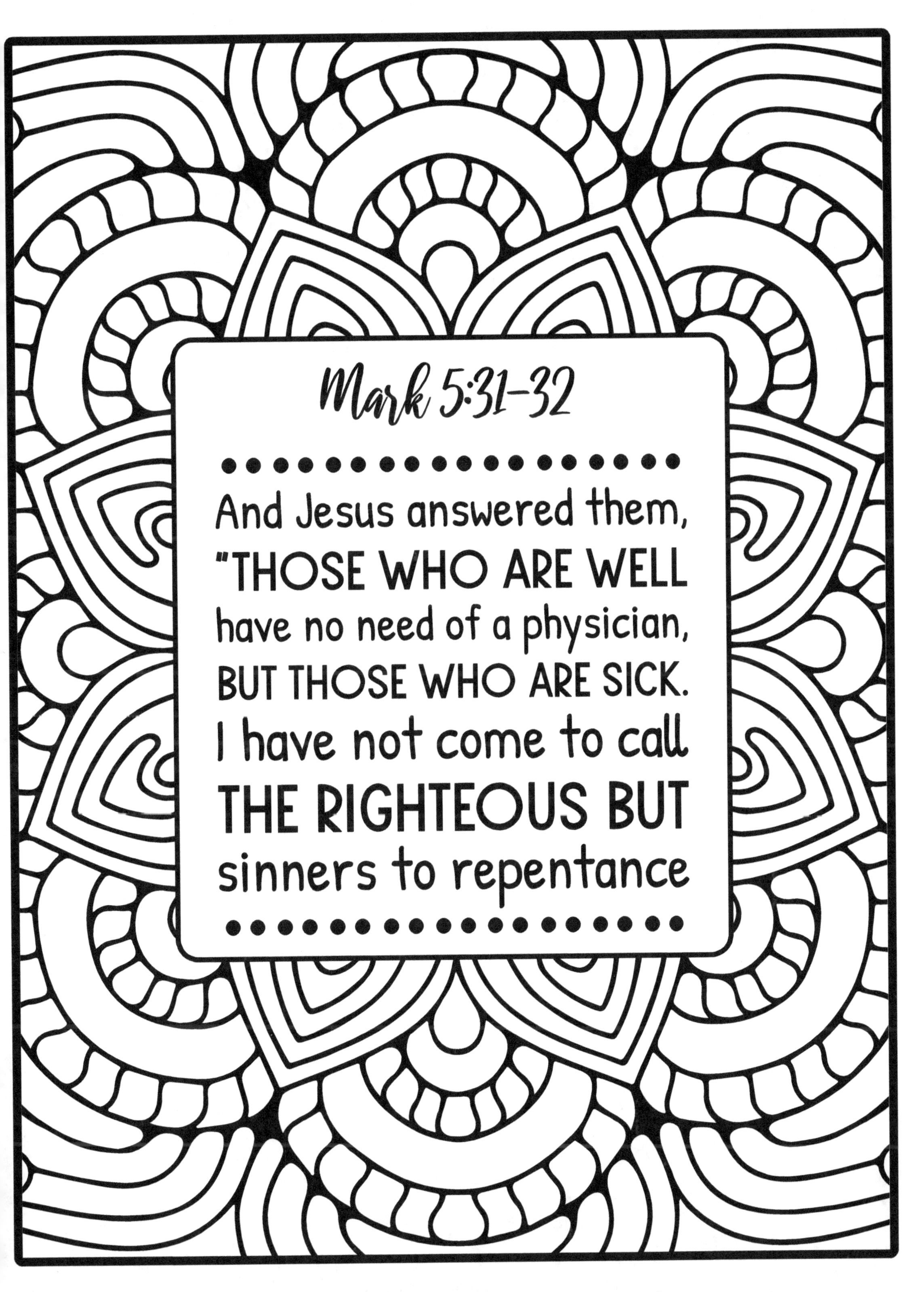
Mark 5:31-32

And Jesus answered them,
"THOSE WHO ARE WELL
have no need of a physician,
BUT THOSE WHO ARE SICK.
I have not come to call
THE RIGHTEOUS BUT
sinners to repentance

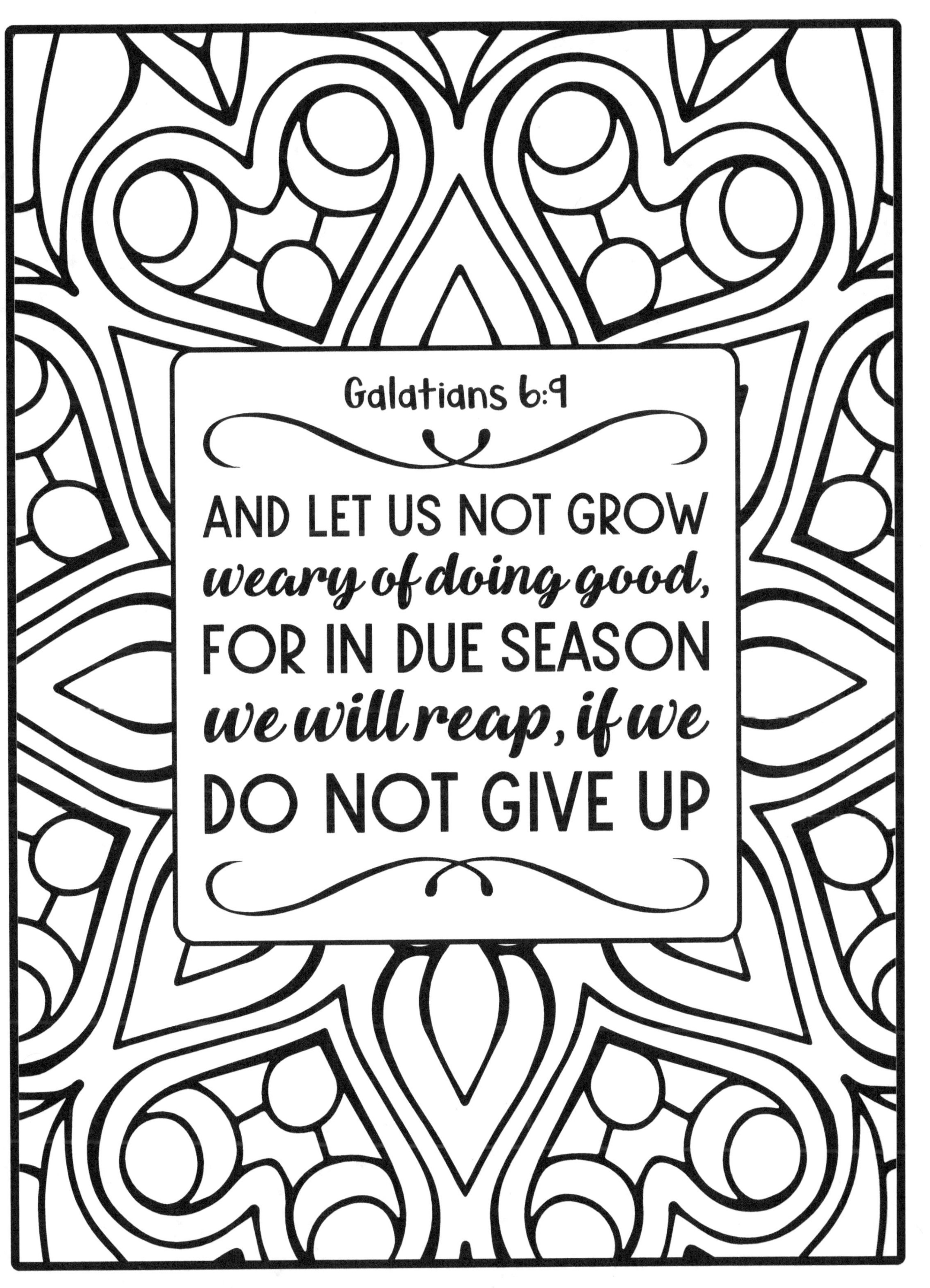

Galatians 6:9
AND LET US NOT GROW weary of doing good, FOR IN DUE SEASON we will reap, if we DO NOT GIVE UP

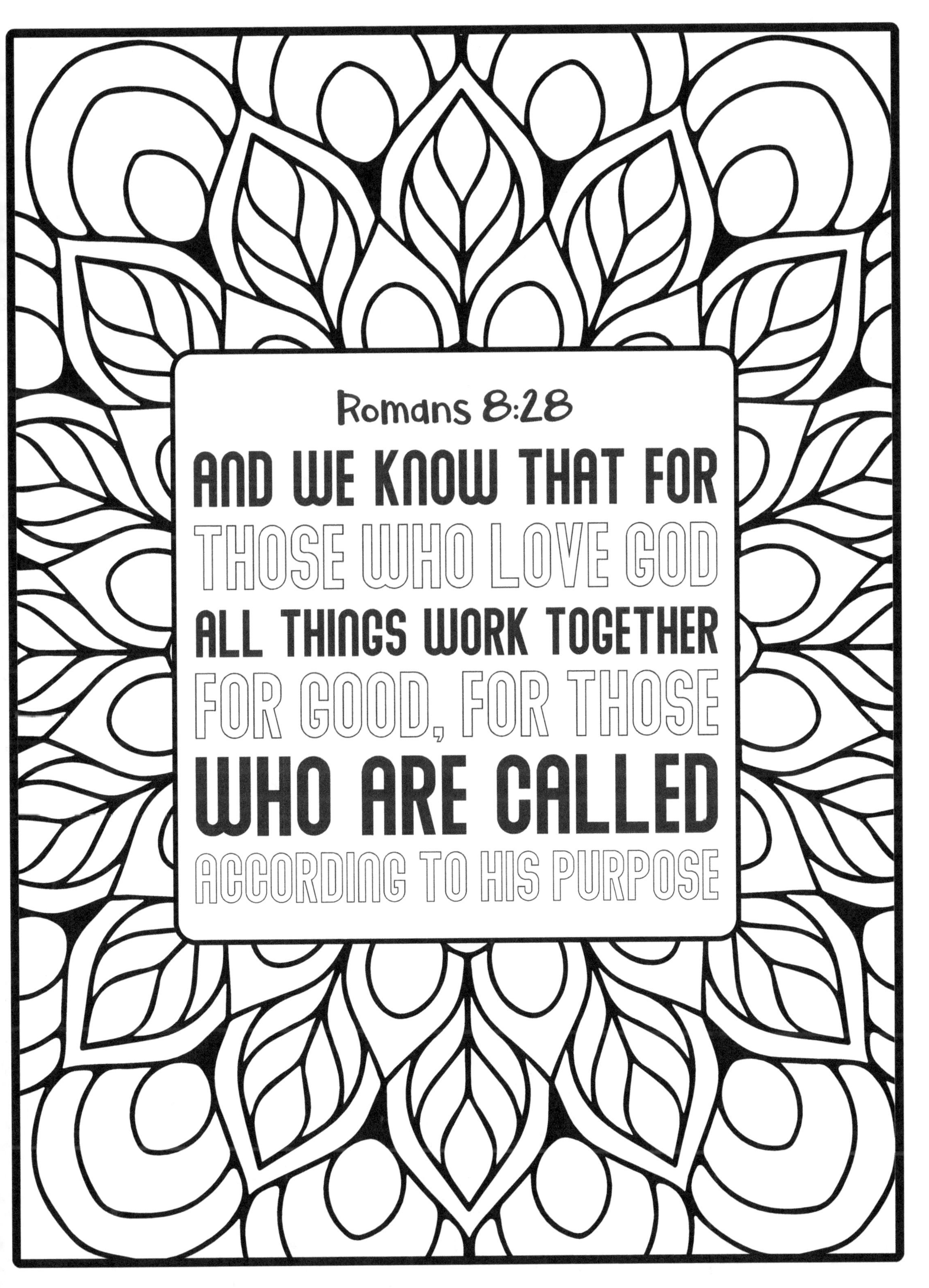

Romans 8:28
AND WE KNOW THAT FOR THOSE WHO LOVE GOD ALL THINGS WORK TOGETHER FOR GOOD, FOR THOSE WHO ARE CALLED ACCORDING TO HIS PURPOSE

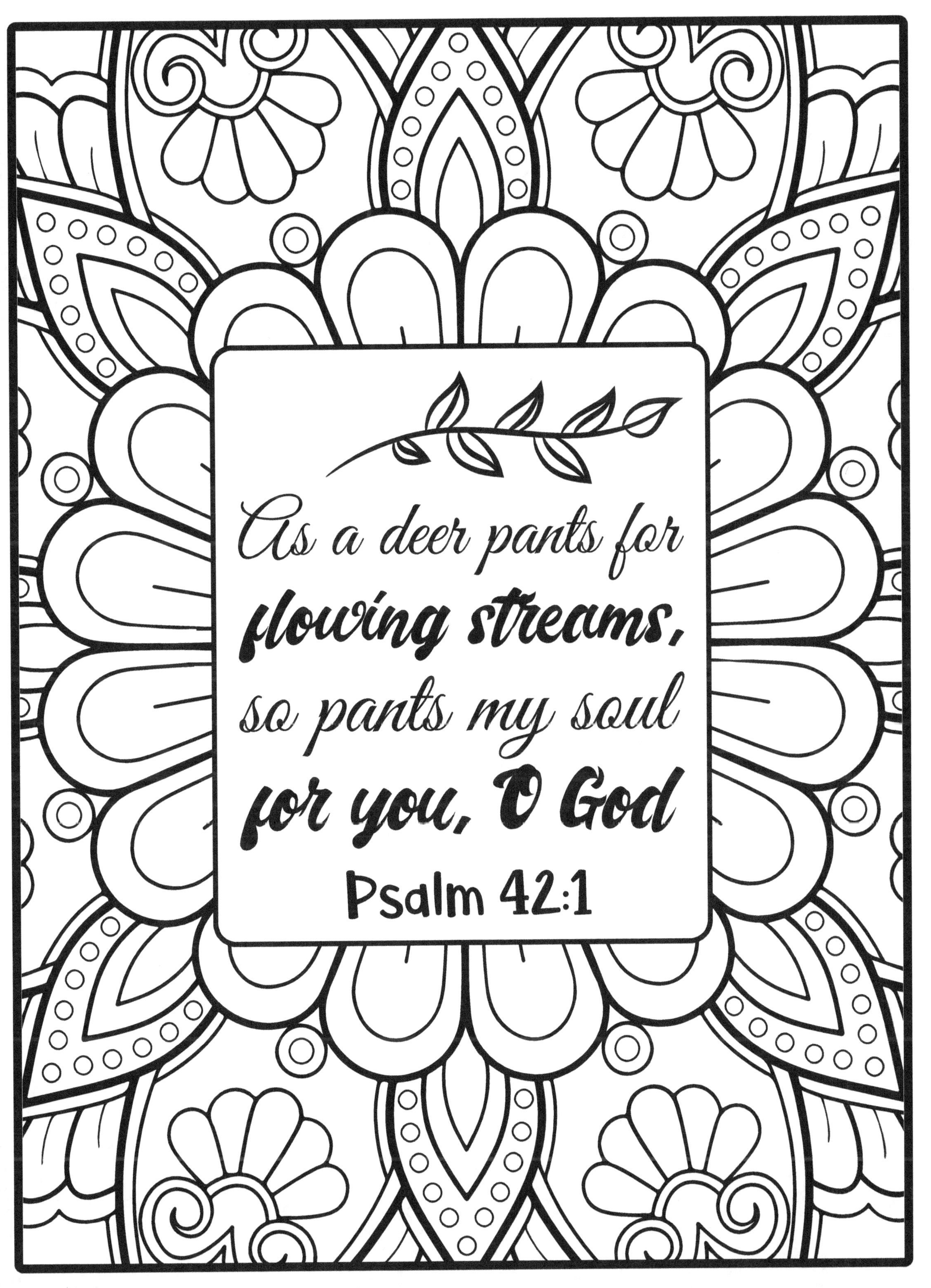
As a deer pants for
flowing streams,
so pants my soul
for you, O God
Psalm 42:1

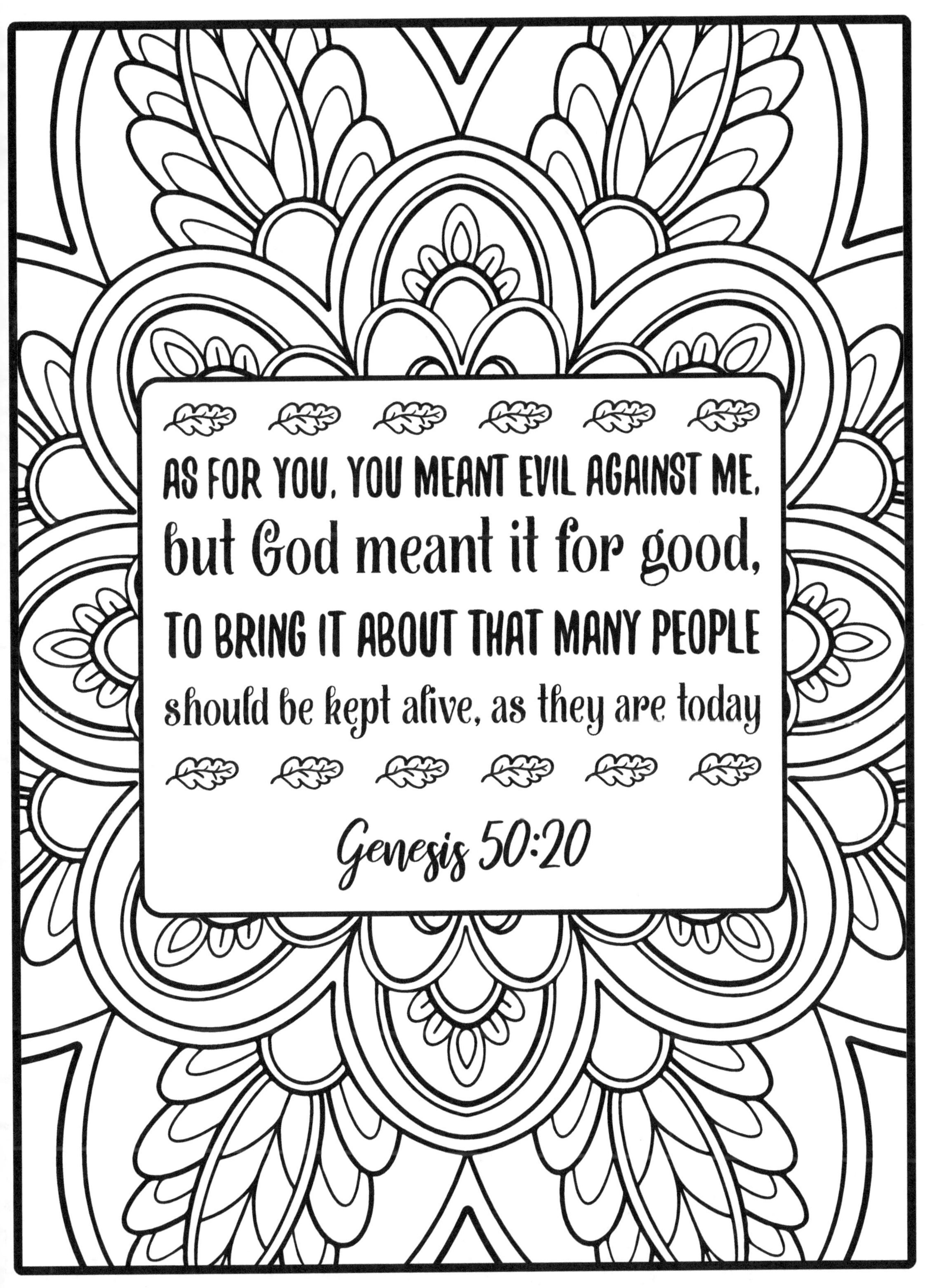
AS FOR YOU, YOU MEANT EVIL AGAINST ME,
but God meant it for good,
TO BRING IT ABOUT THAT MANY PEOPLE
should be kept alive, as they are today
Genesis 50:20

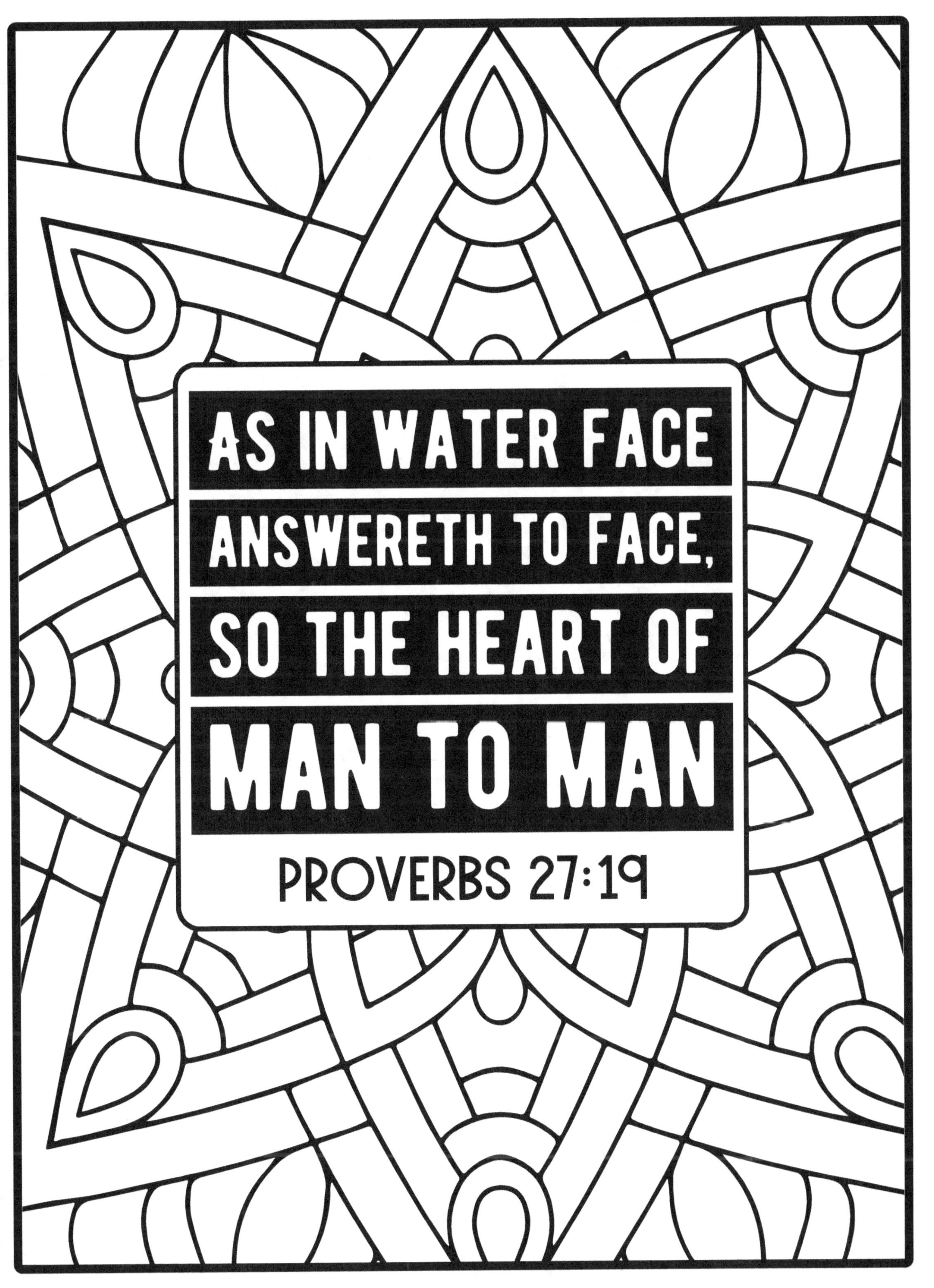

As in water face
answereth to face,
so the heart of
man to man
Proverbs 27:19

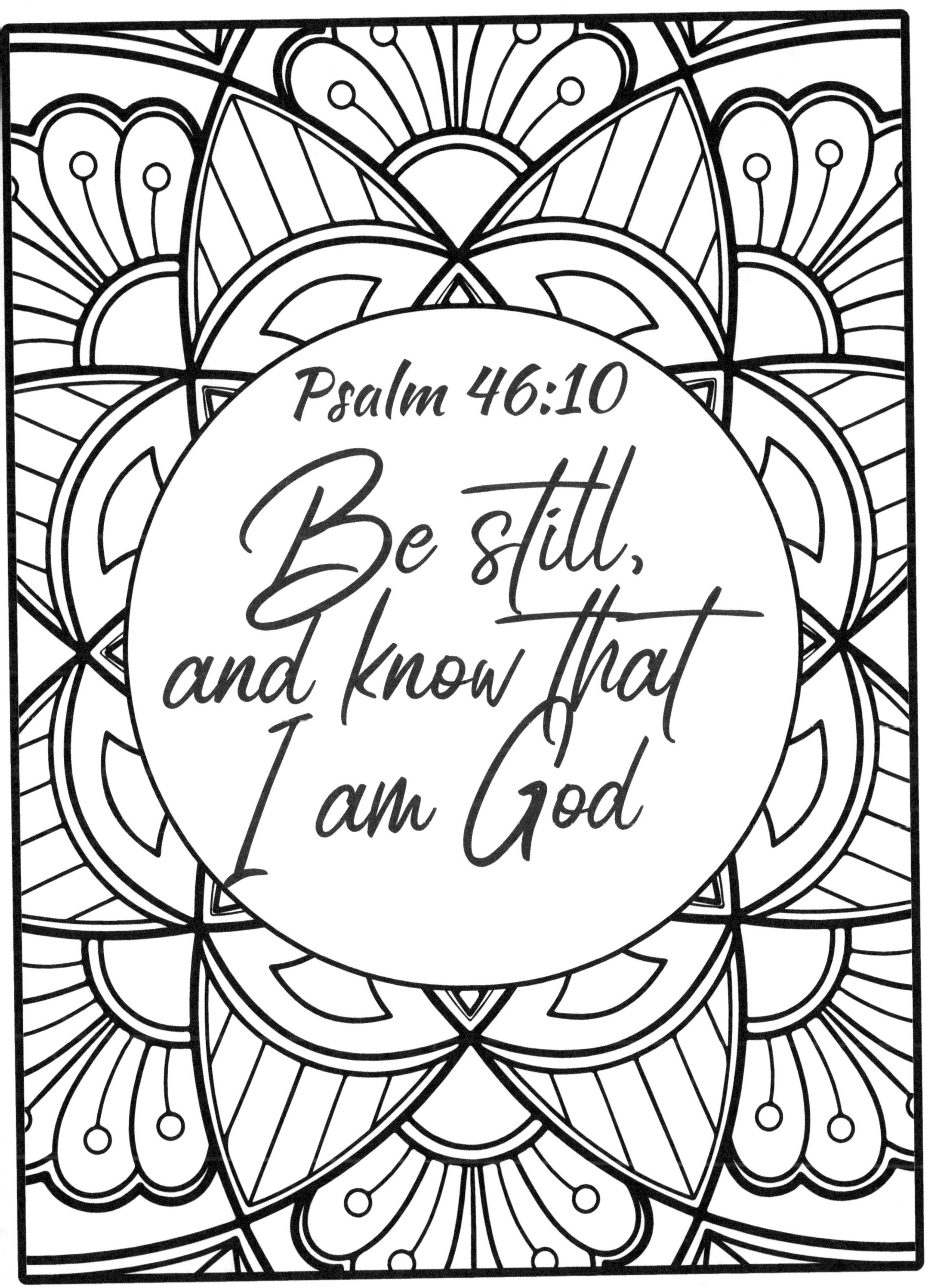

Psalm 46:10
Be still,
and know that
I am God

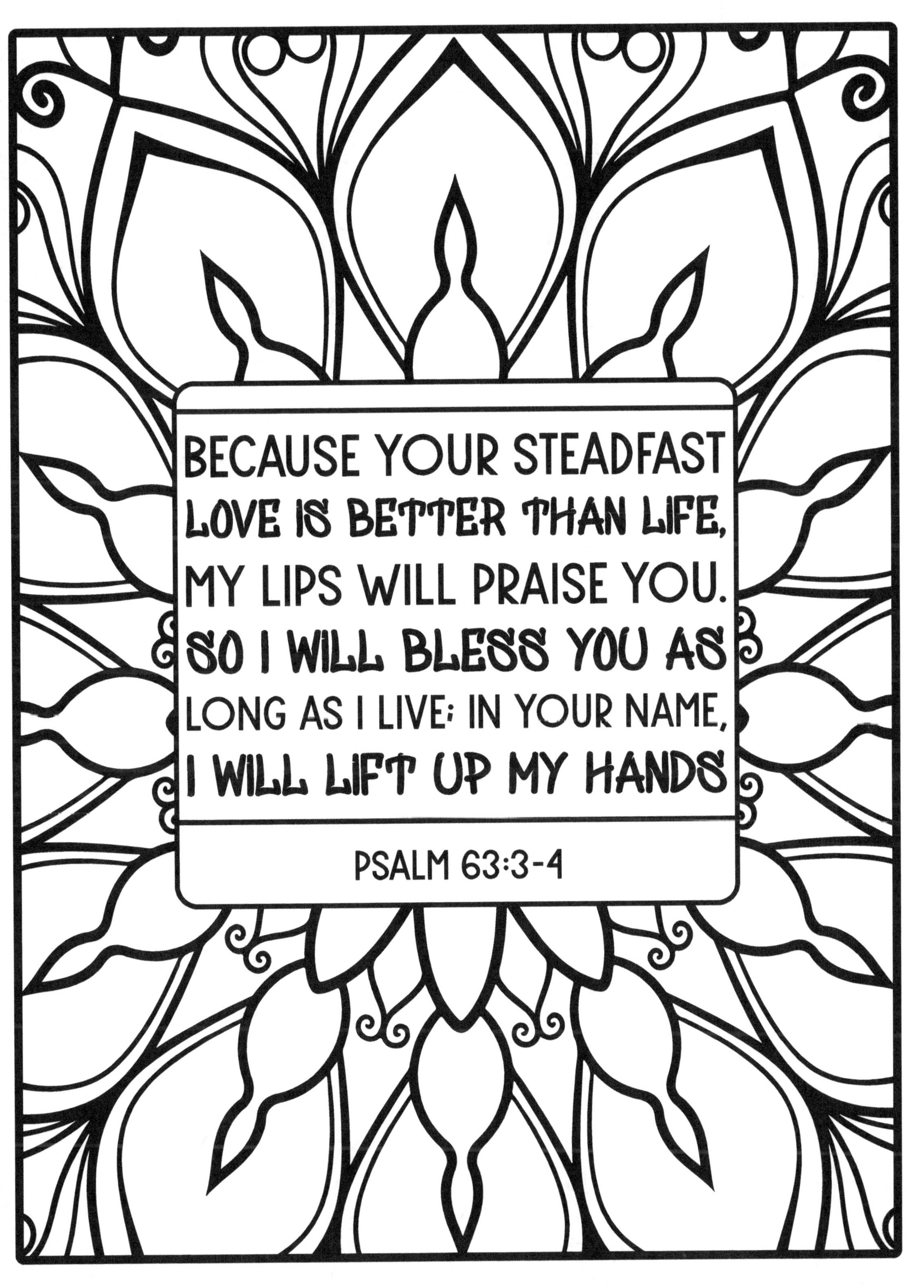
BECAUSE YOUR STEADFAST
LOVE IS BETTER THAN LIFE,
MY LIPS WILL PRAISE YOU.
SO I WILL BLESS YOU AS
LONG AS I LIVE; IN YOUR NAME,
I WILL LIFT UP MY HANDS

PSALM 63:3-4

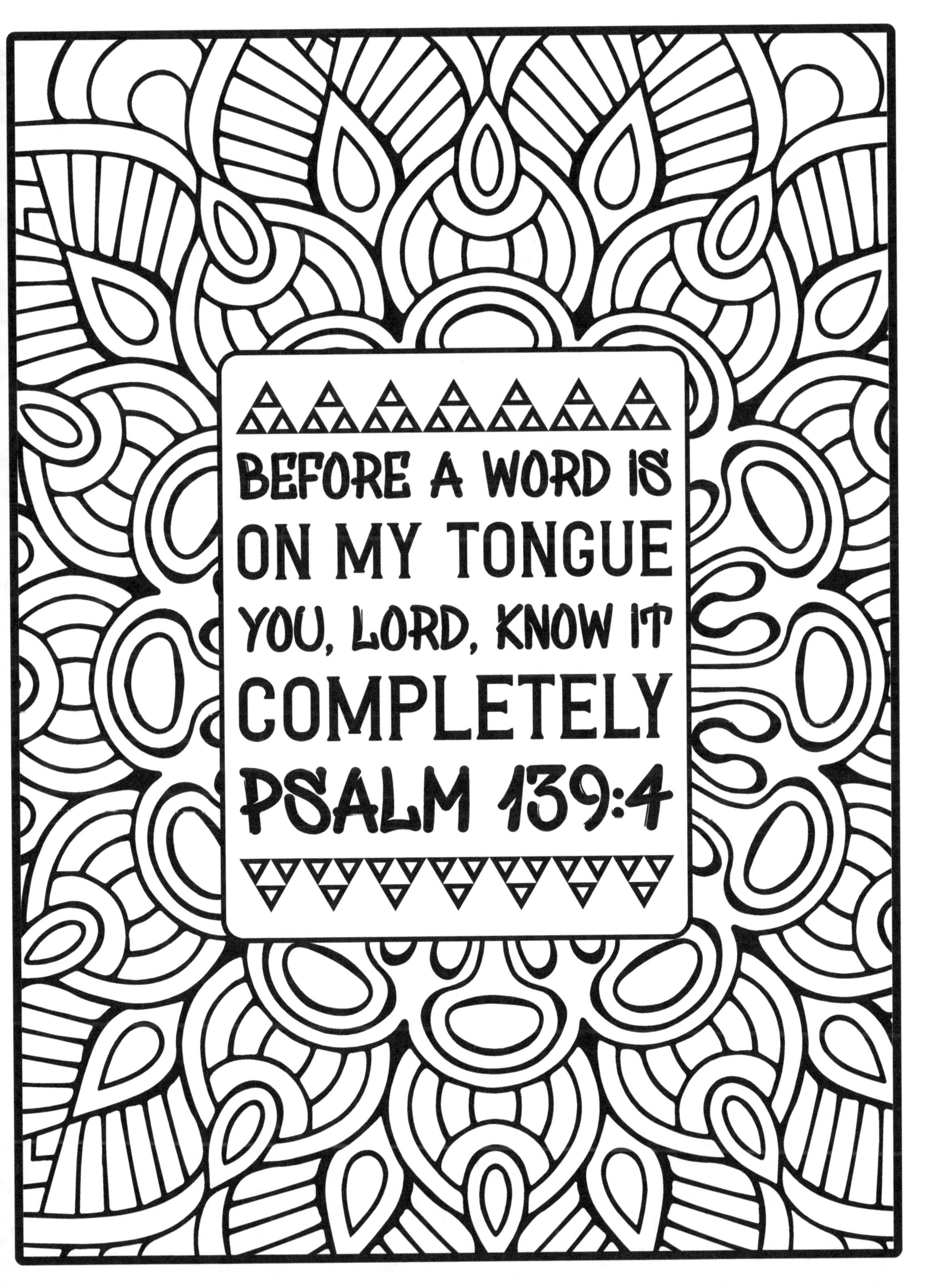

BEFORE A WORD IS
ON MY TONGUE
YOU, LORD, KNOW IT
COMPLETELY
PSALM 139:4

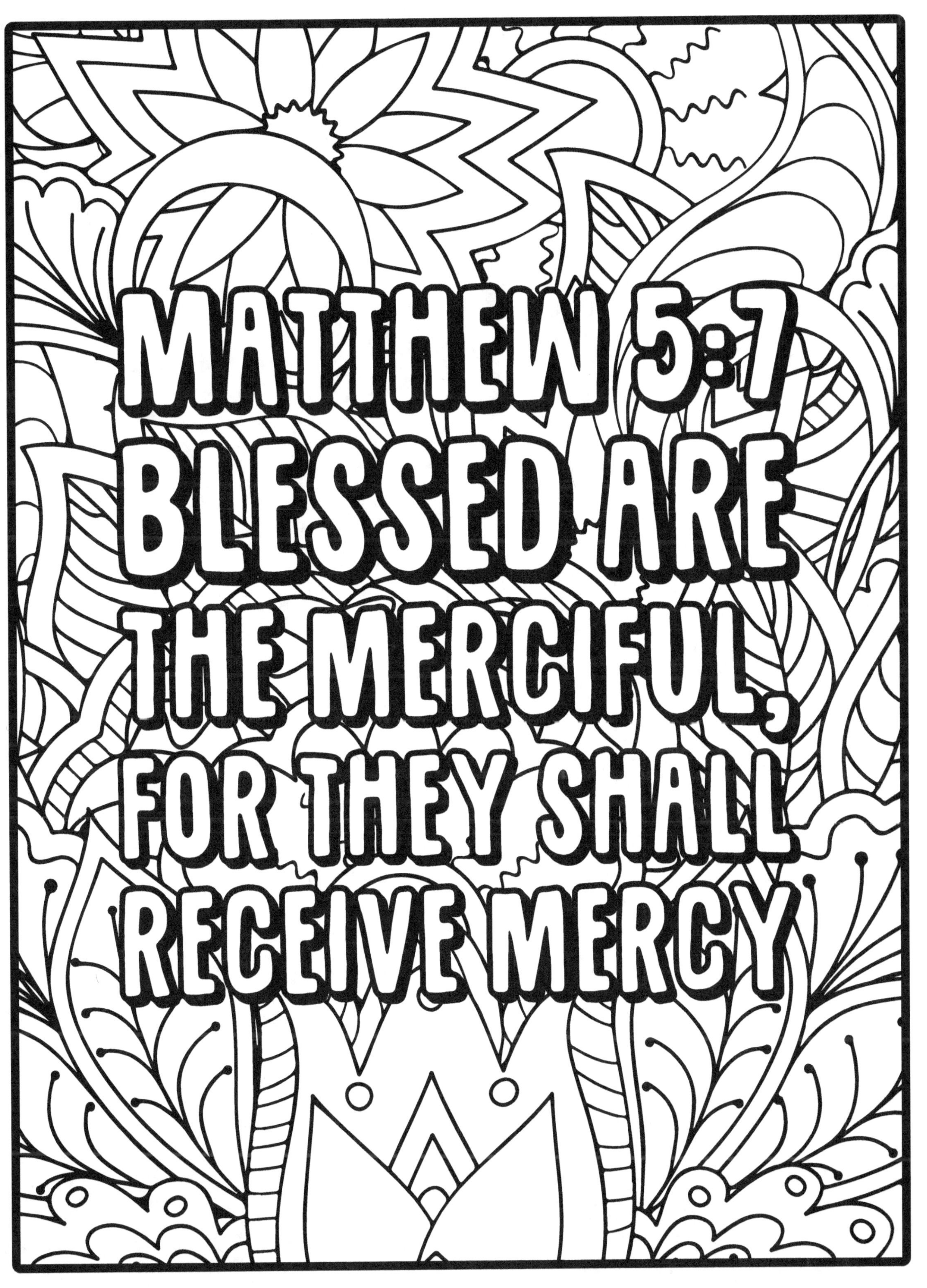

MATTHEW 5:7
BLESSED ARE
THE MERCIFUL,
FOR THEY SHALL
RECEIVE MERCY

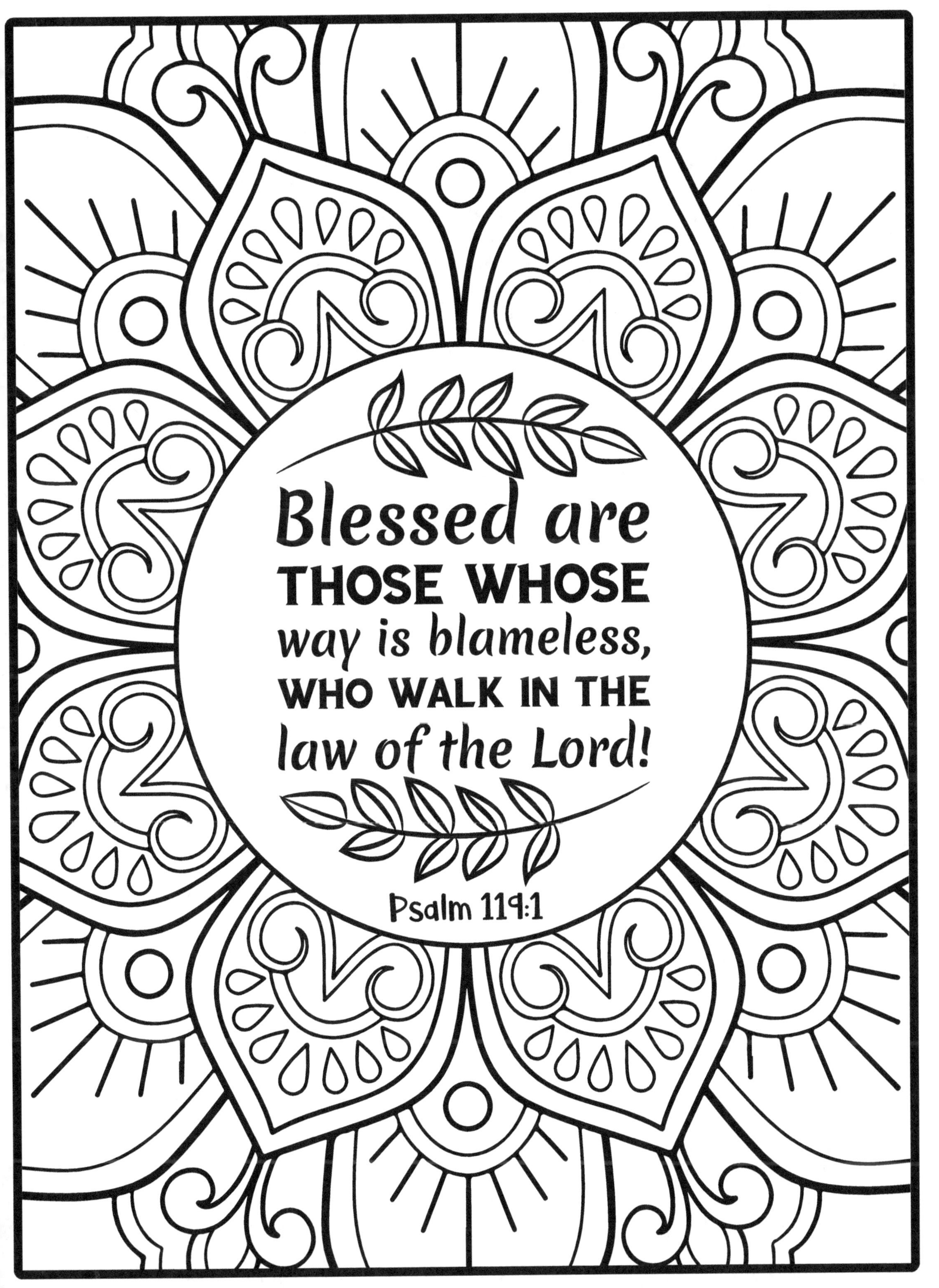

Blessed are
THOSE WHOSE
way is blameless,
WHO WALK IN THE
law of the Lord!
Psalm 119:1

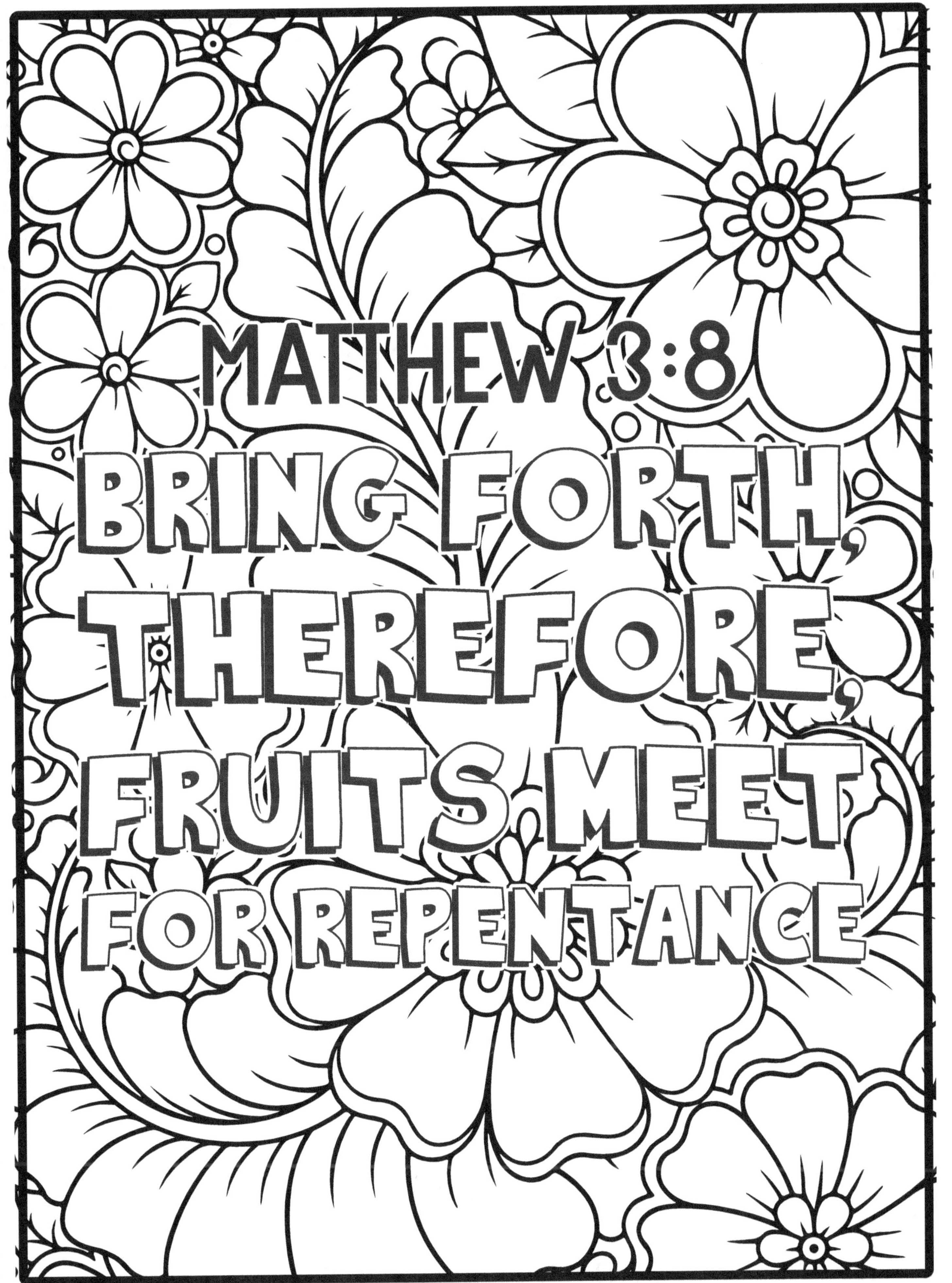
MATTHEW 3:8
BRING FORTH, THEREFORE, FRUITS MEET FOR REPENTANCE

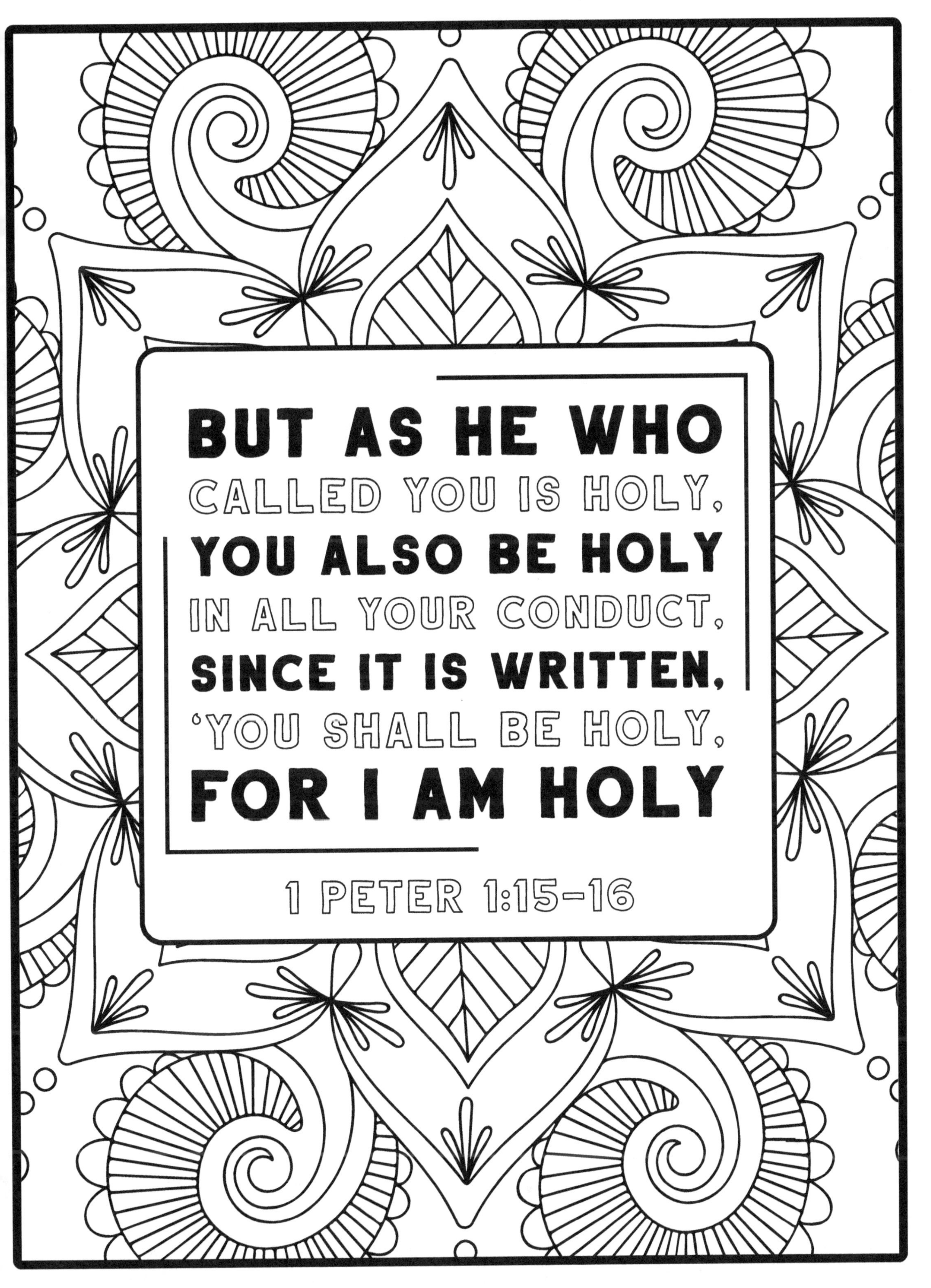

BUT AS HE WHO
CALLED YOU IS HOLY,
YOU ALSO BE HOLY
IN ALL YOUR CONDUCT,
SINCE IT IS WRITTEN,
'YOU SHALL BE HOLY,
FOR I AM HOLY
1 PETER 1:15-16

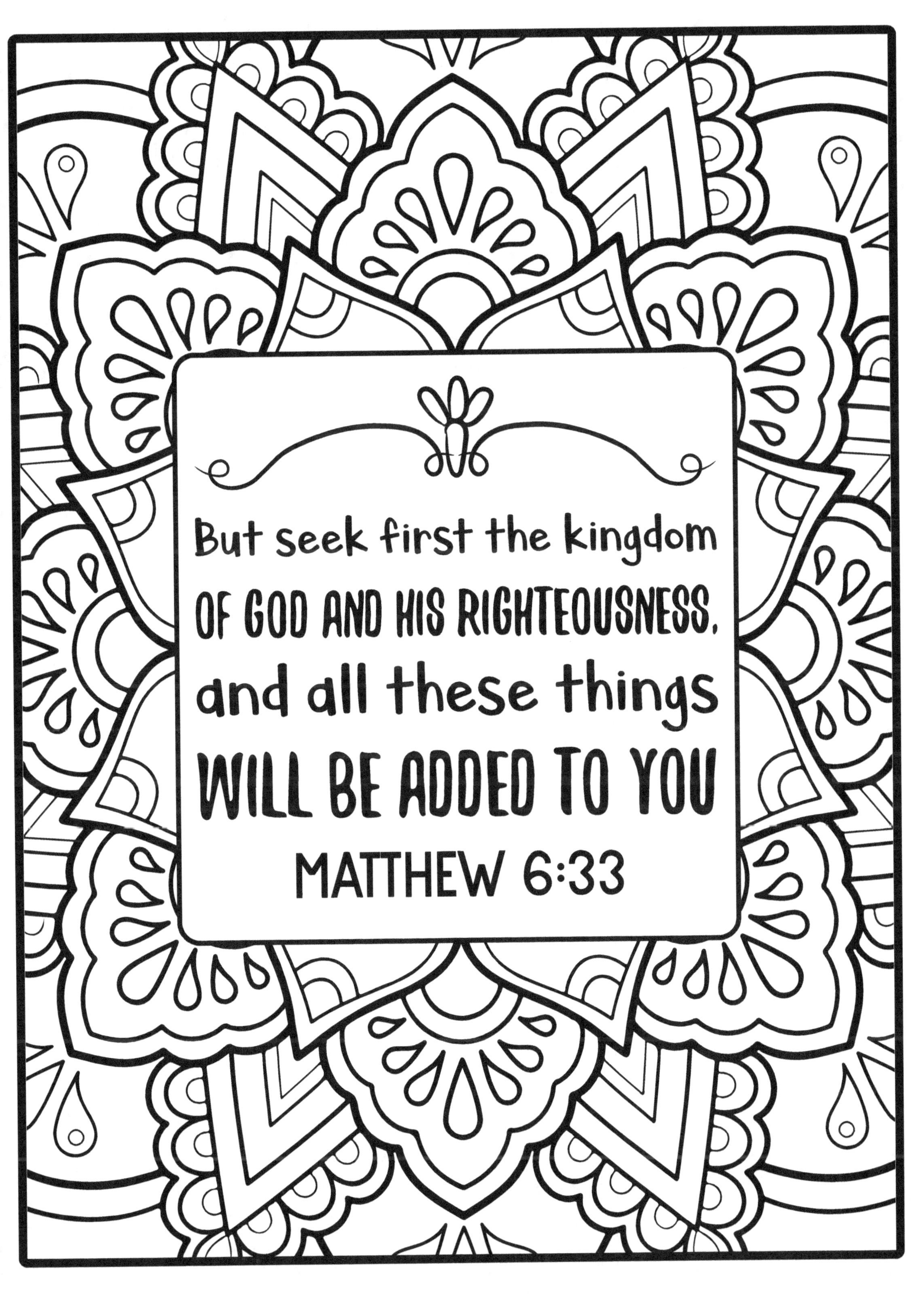

But seek first the kingdom
OF GOD AND HIS RIGHTEOUSNESS,
and all these things
WILL BE ADDED TO YOU
MATTHEW 6:33

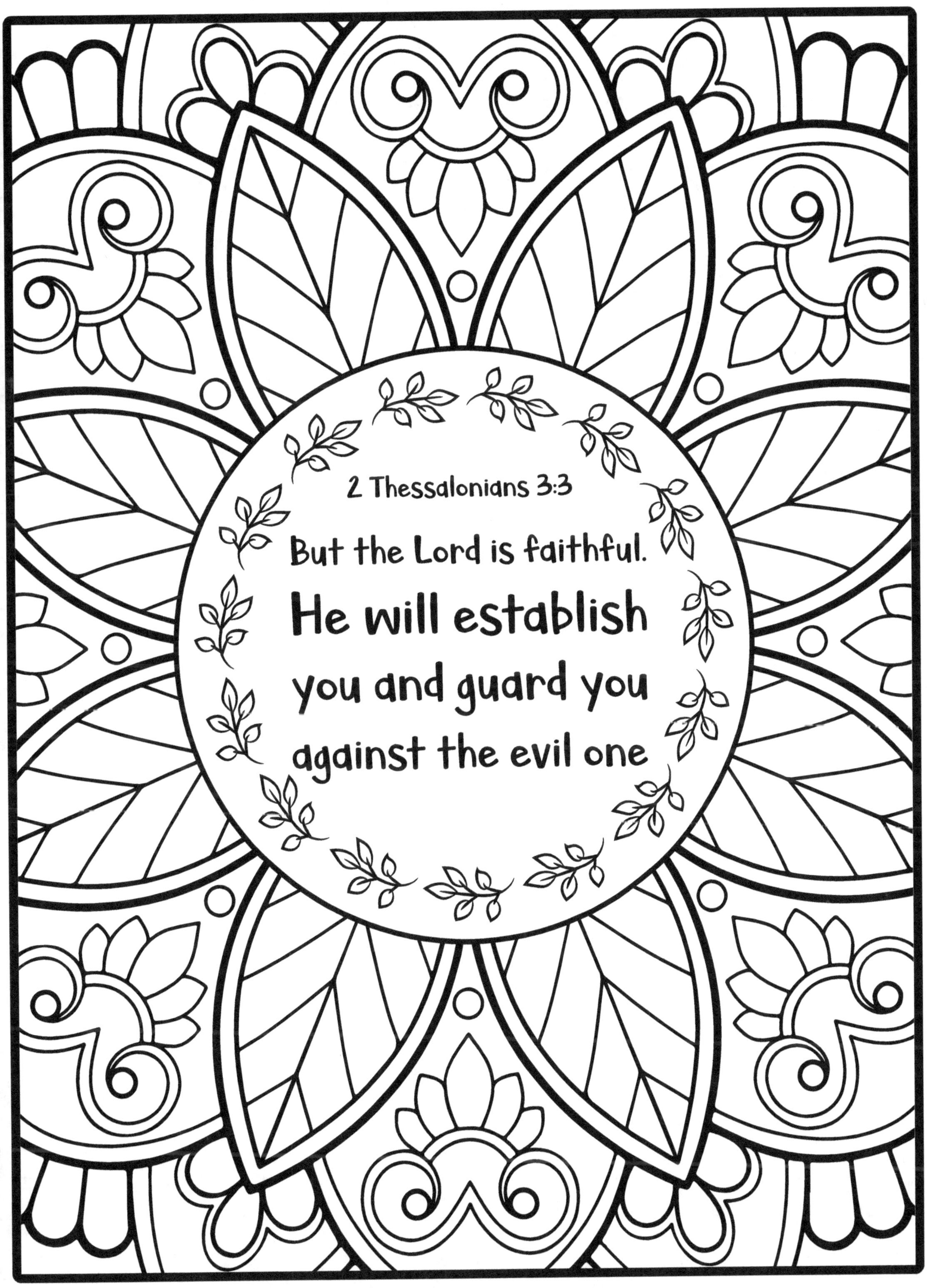

2 Thessalonians 3:3

But the Lord is faithful.
He will establish
you and guard you
against the evil one

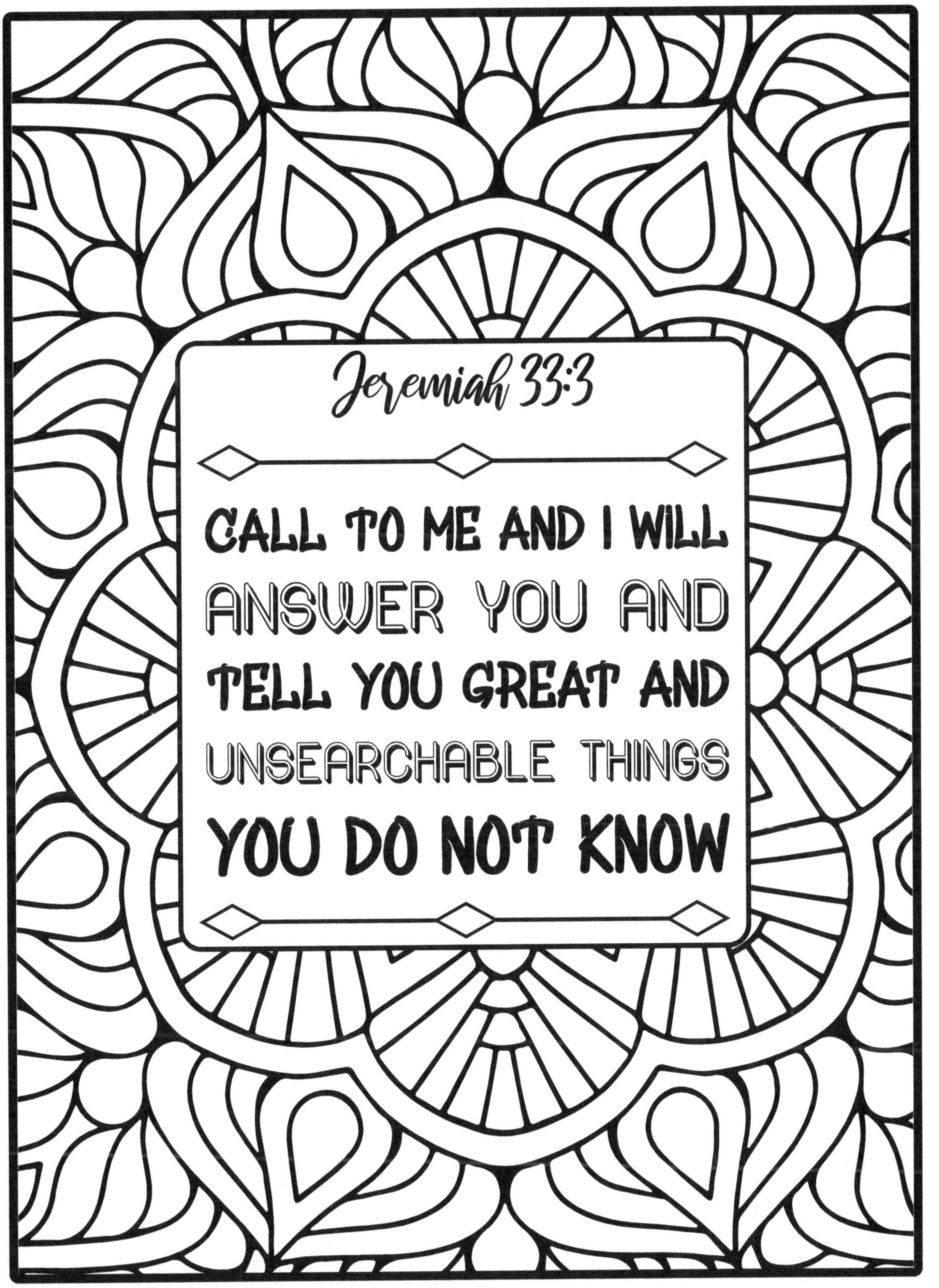

Jeremiah 33:3
CALL TO ME AND I WILL ANSWER YOU AND TELL YOU GREAT AND UNSEARCHABLE THINGS YOU DO NOT KNOW

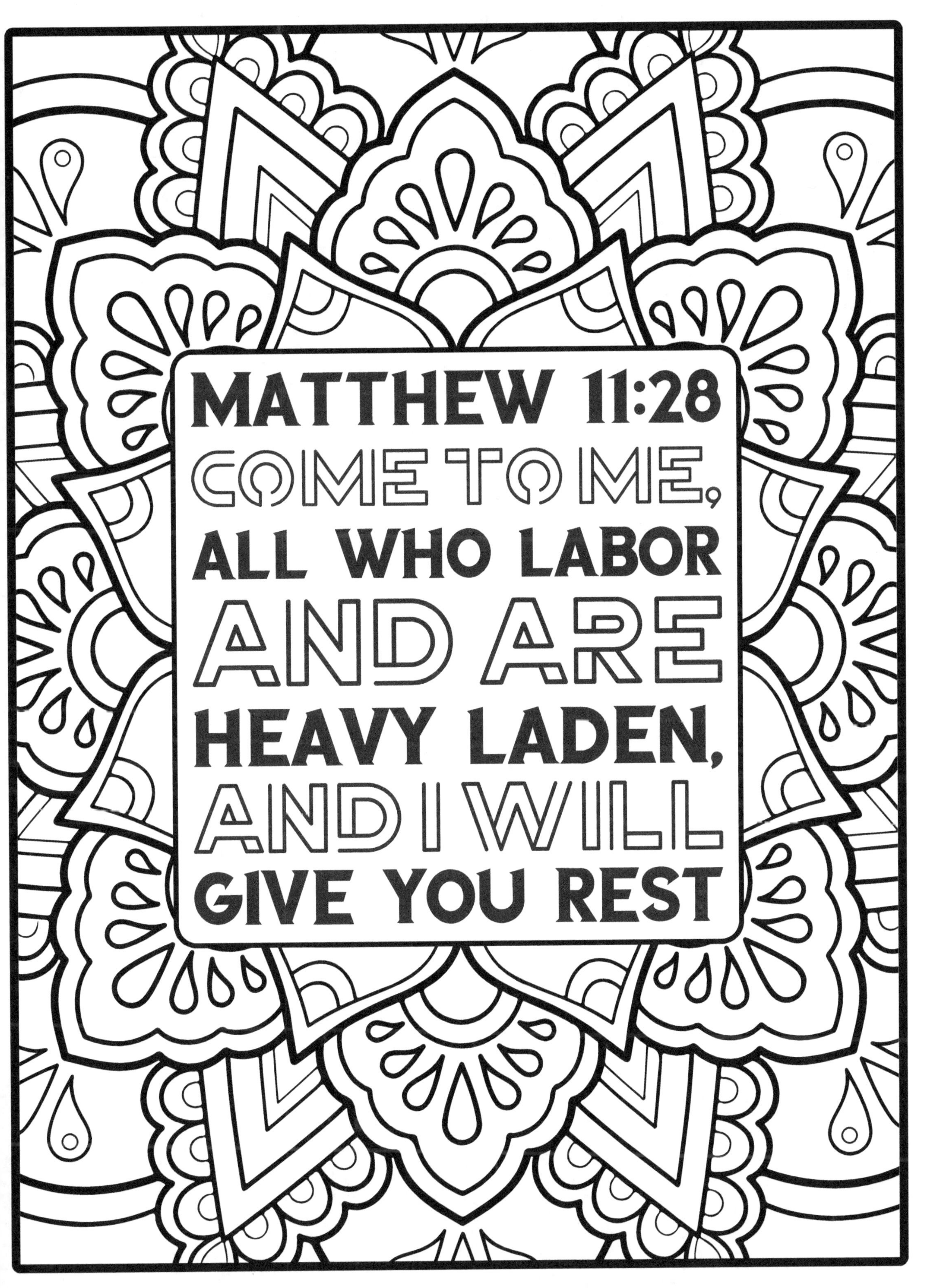

MATTHEW 11:28
COME TO ME,
ALL WHO LABOR
AND ARE
HEAVY LADEN,
AND I WILL
GIVE YOU REST

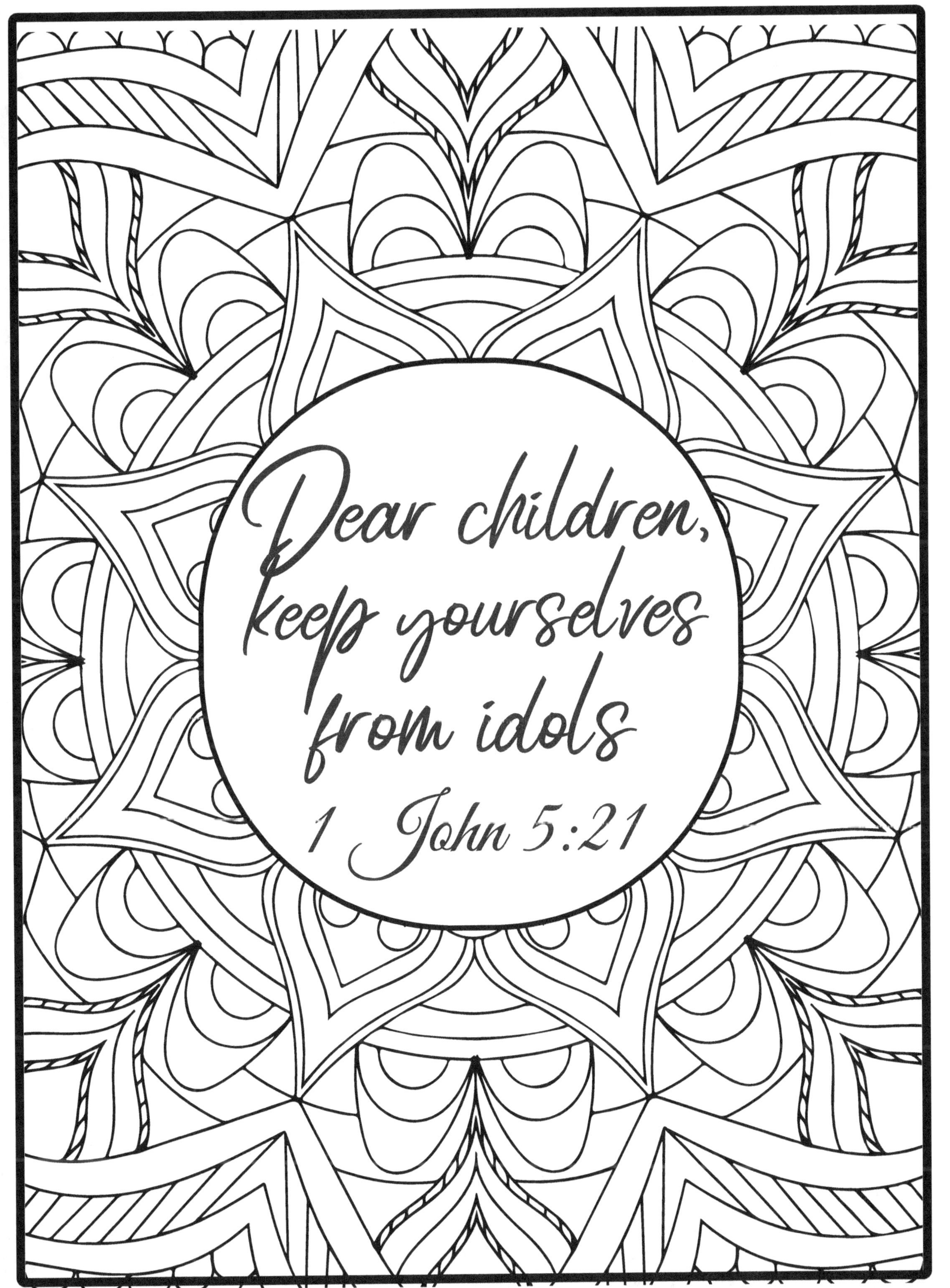

Dear children,
keep yourselves
from idols
1 John 5:21

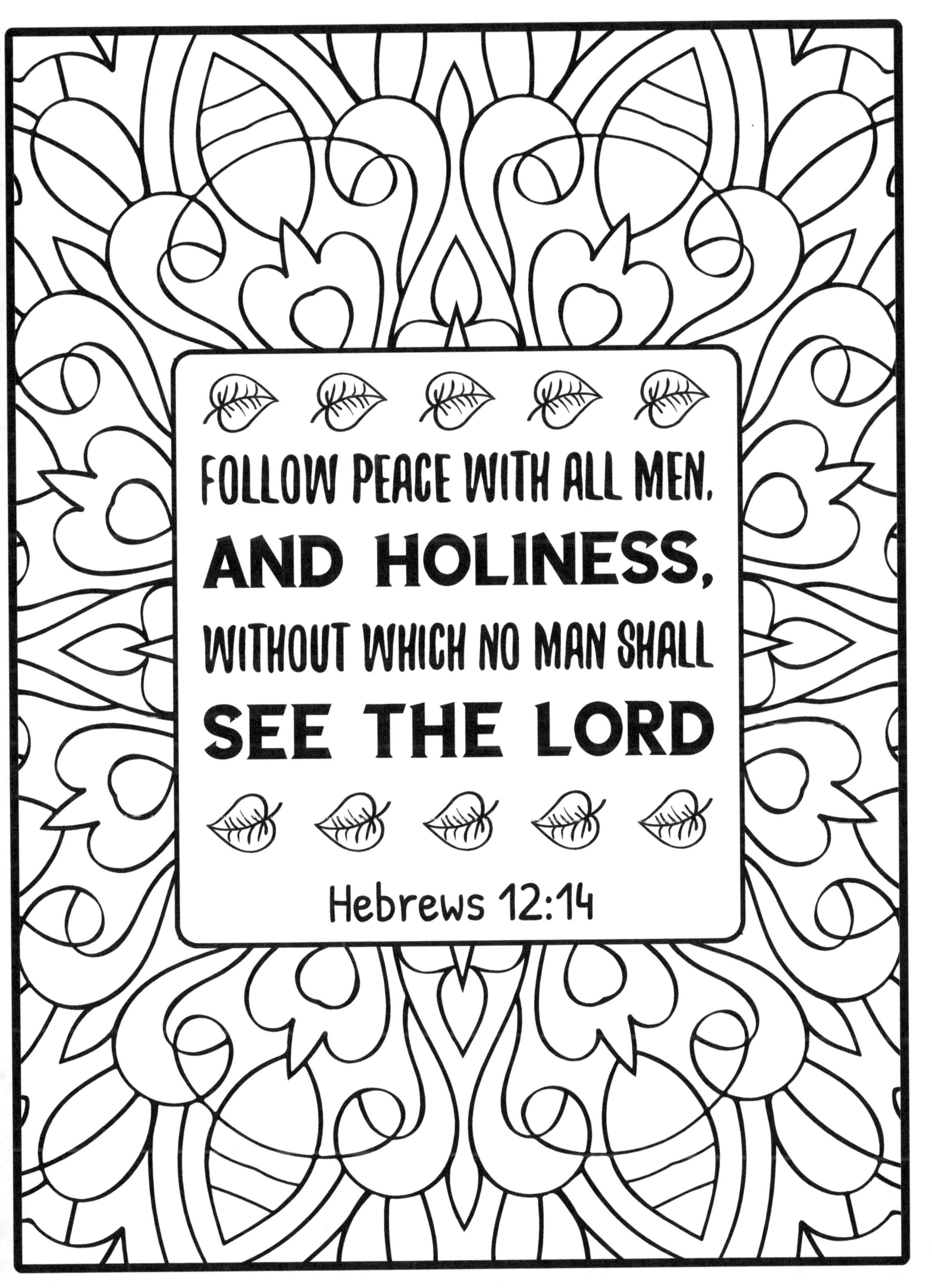

FOLLOW PEACE WITH ALL MEN,
AND HOLINESS,
WITHOUT WHICH NO MAN SHALL
SEE THE LORD
Hebrews 12:14

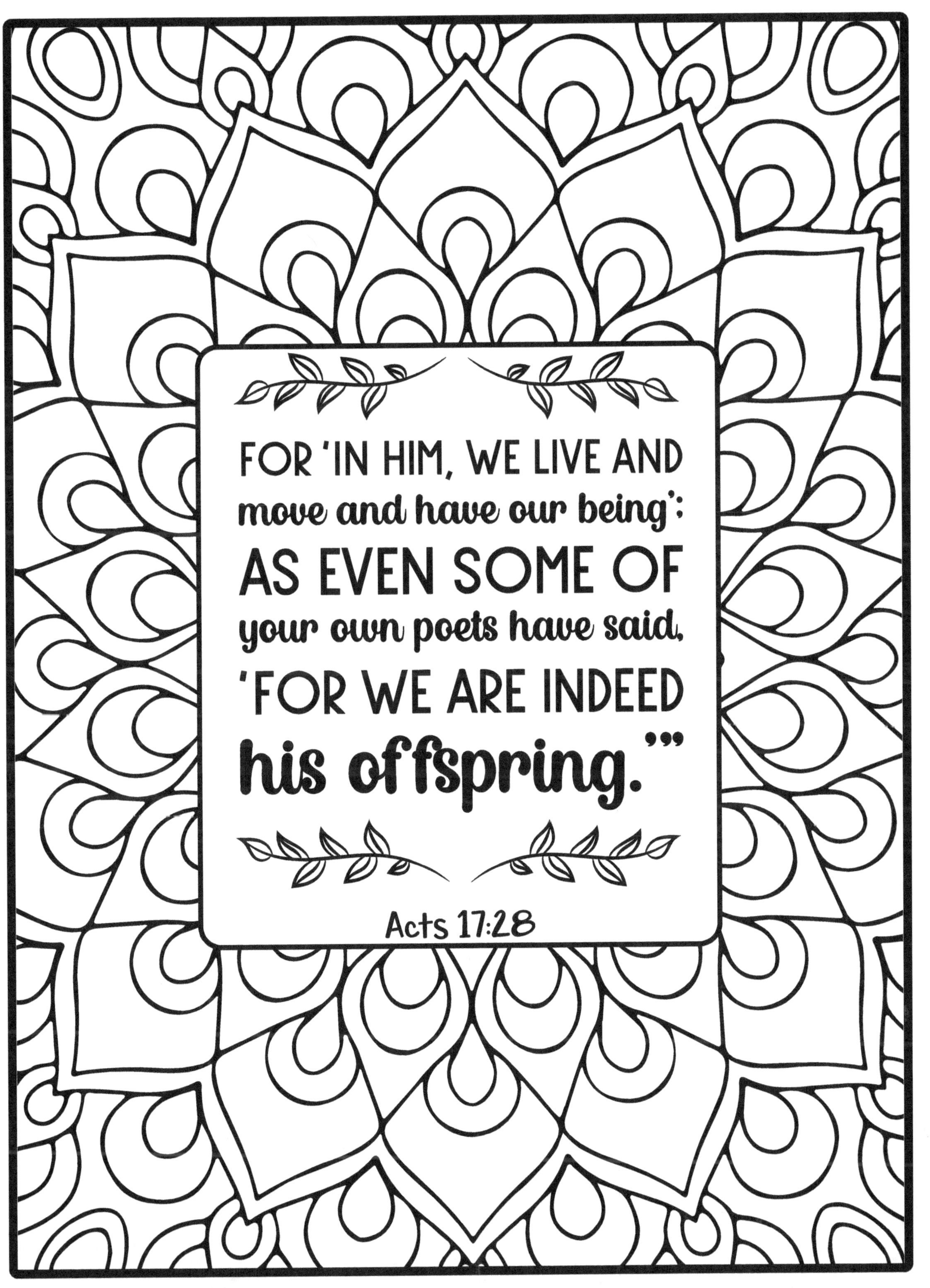

FOR 'IN HIM, WE LIVE AND move and have our being': AS EVEN SOME OF your own poets have said, 'FOR WE ARE INDEED his offspring.'"
Acts 17:28

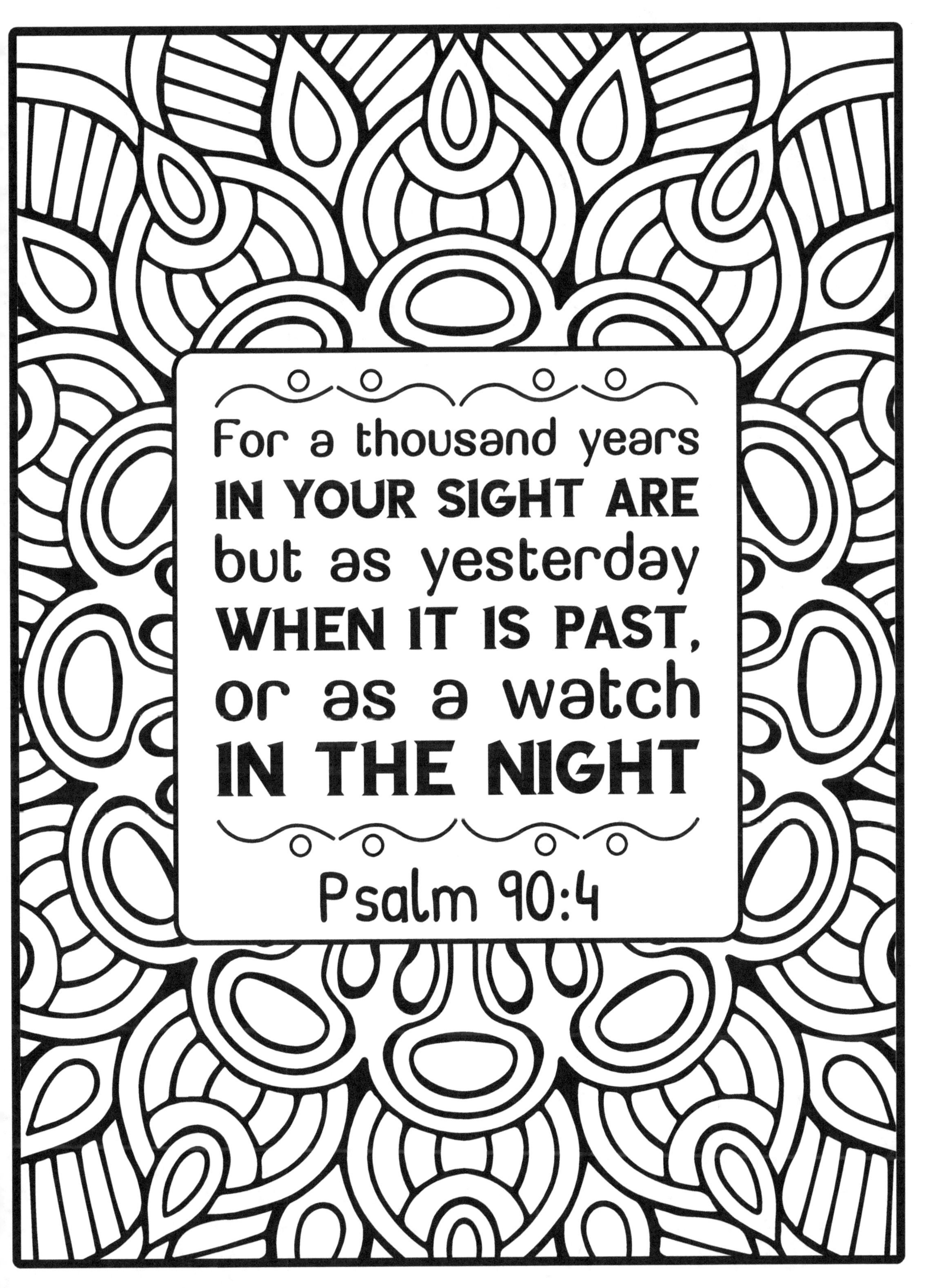

For a thousand years
IN YOUR SIGHT ARE
but as yesterday
WHEN IT IS PAST,
or as a watch
IN THE NIGHT
Psalm 90:4

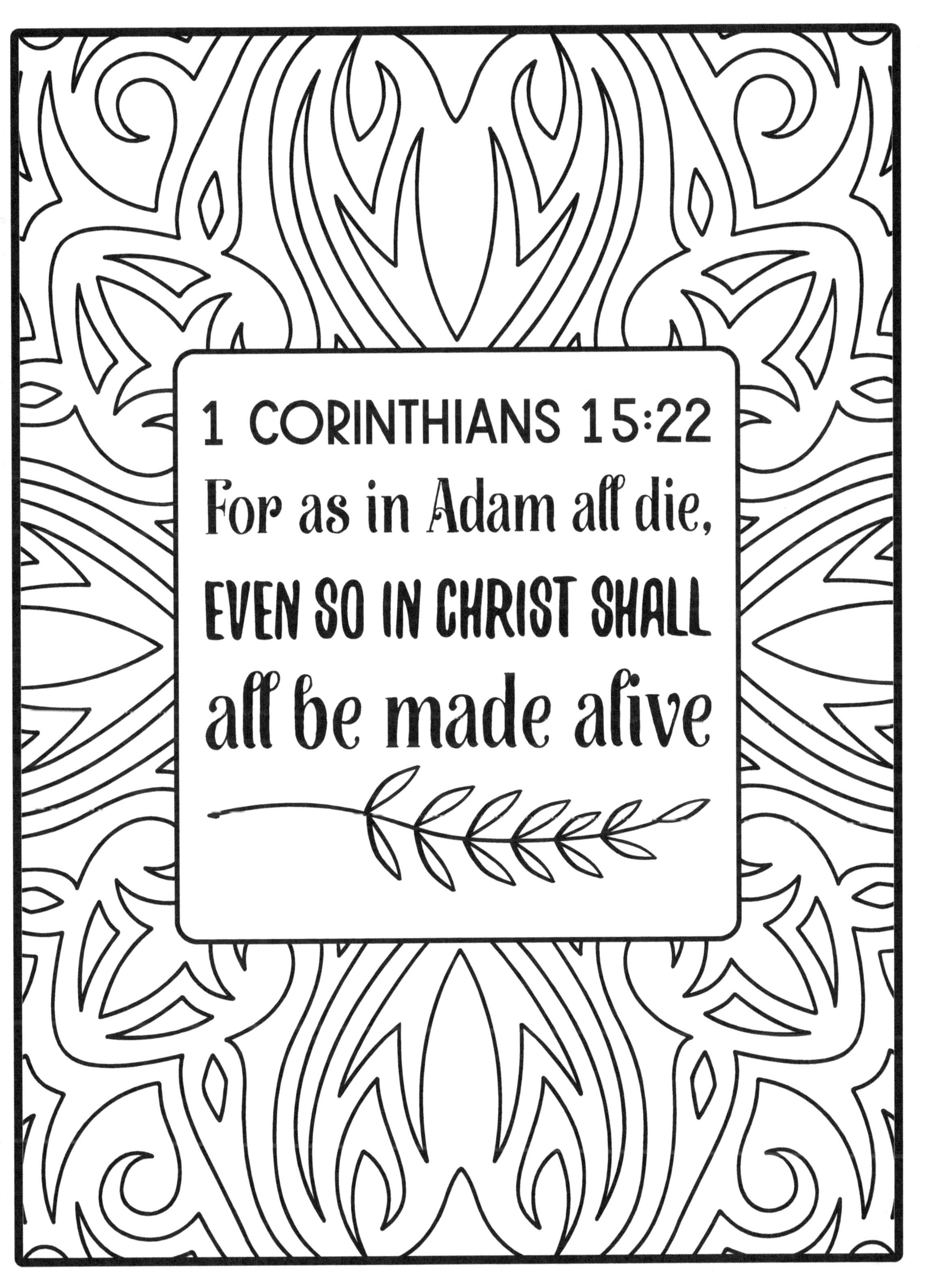

1 CORINTHIANS 15:22
For as in Adam all die,
EVEN SO IN CHRIST SHALL
all be made alive

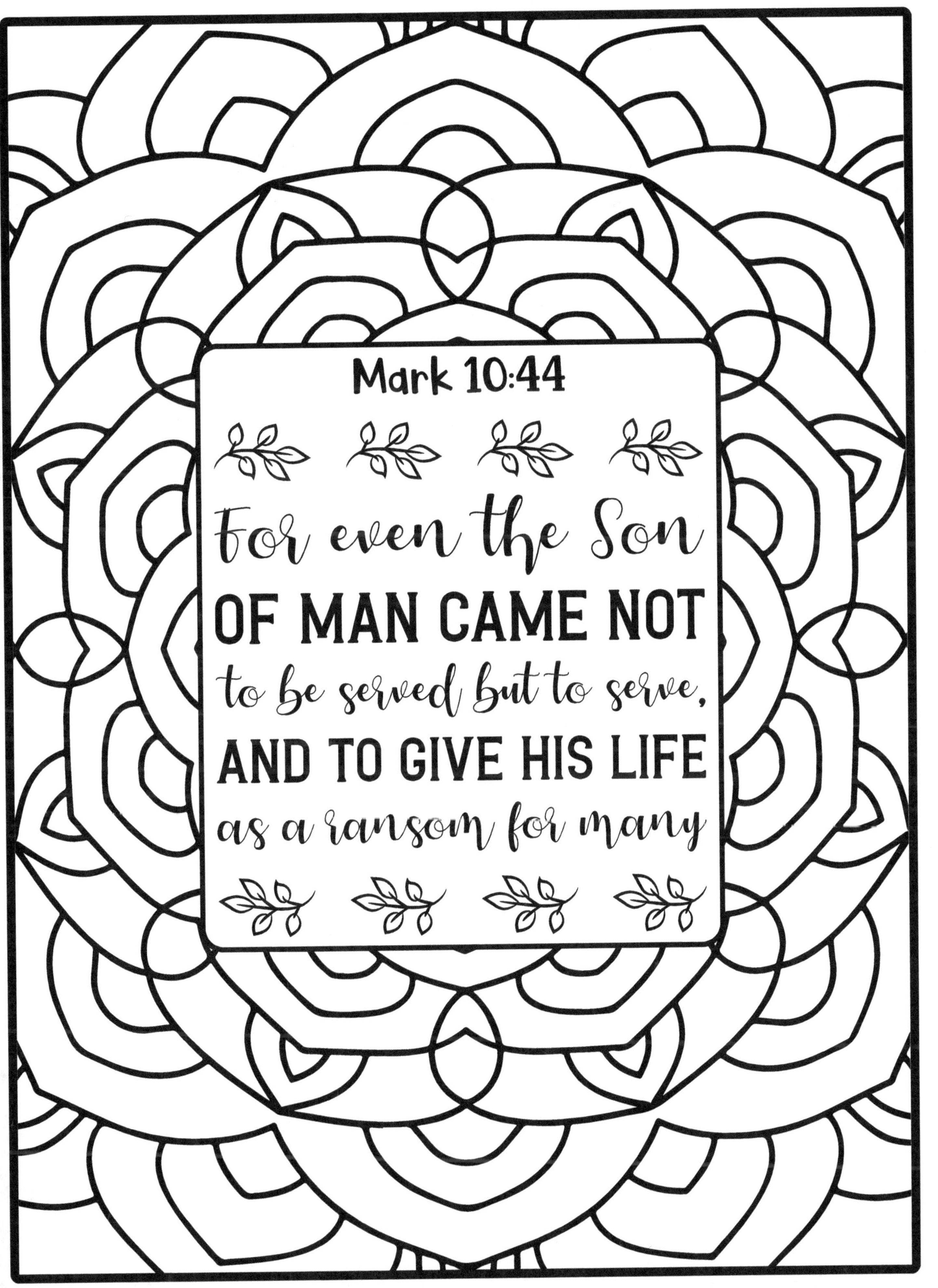

Mark 10:44
For even the Son OF MAN CAME NOT to be served but to serve, AND TO GIVE HIS LIFE as a ransom for many

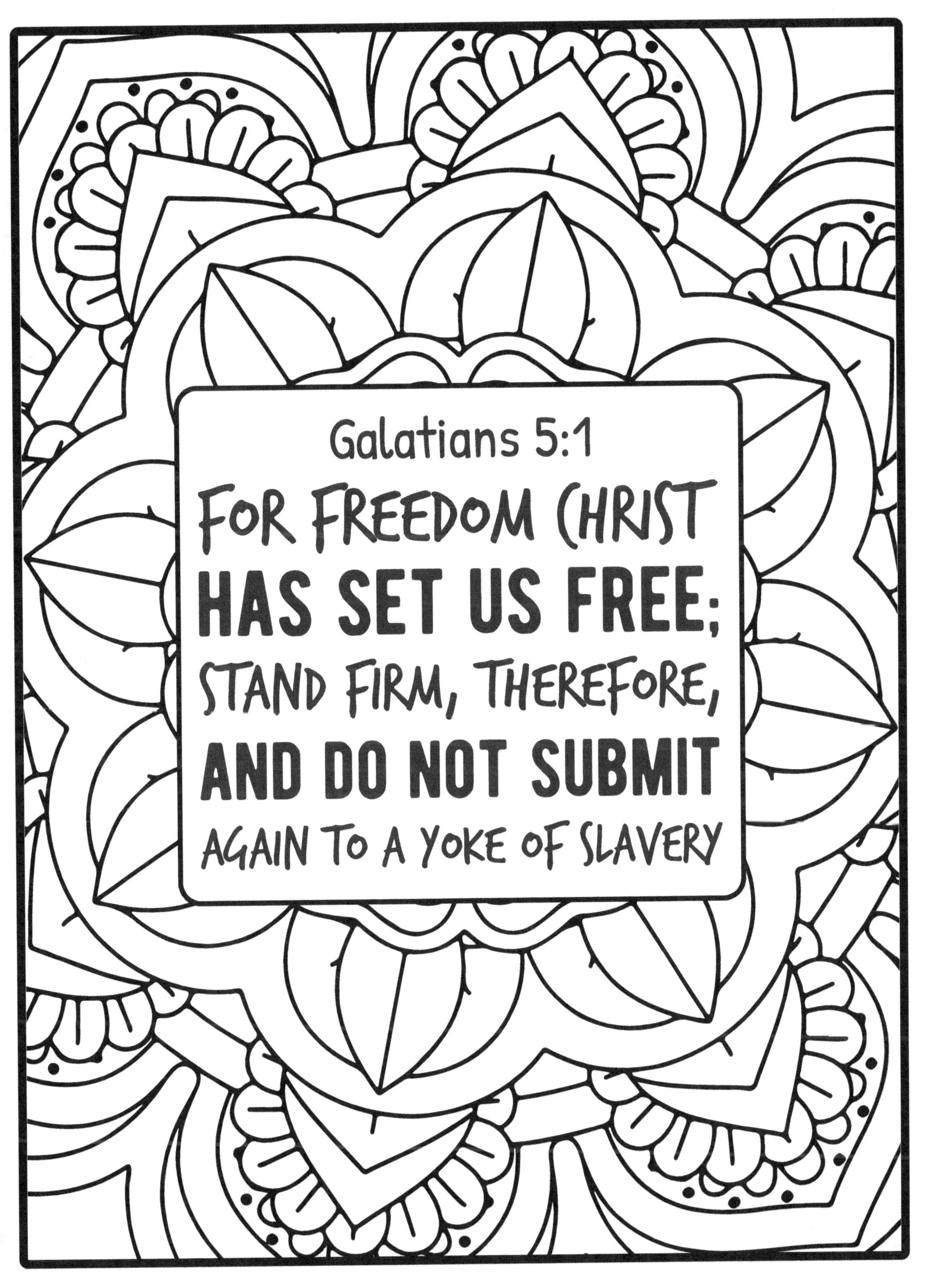

Galatians 5:1
FOR FREEDOM CHRIST HAS SET US FREE; STAND FIRM, THEREFORE, AND DO NOT SUBMIT AGAIN TO A YOKE OF SLAVERY

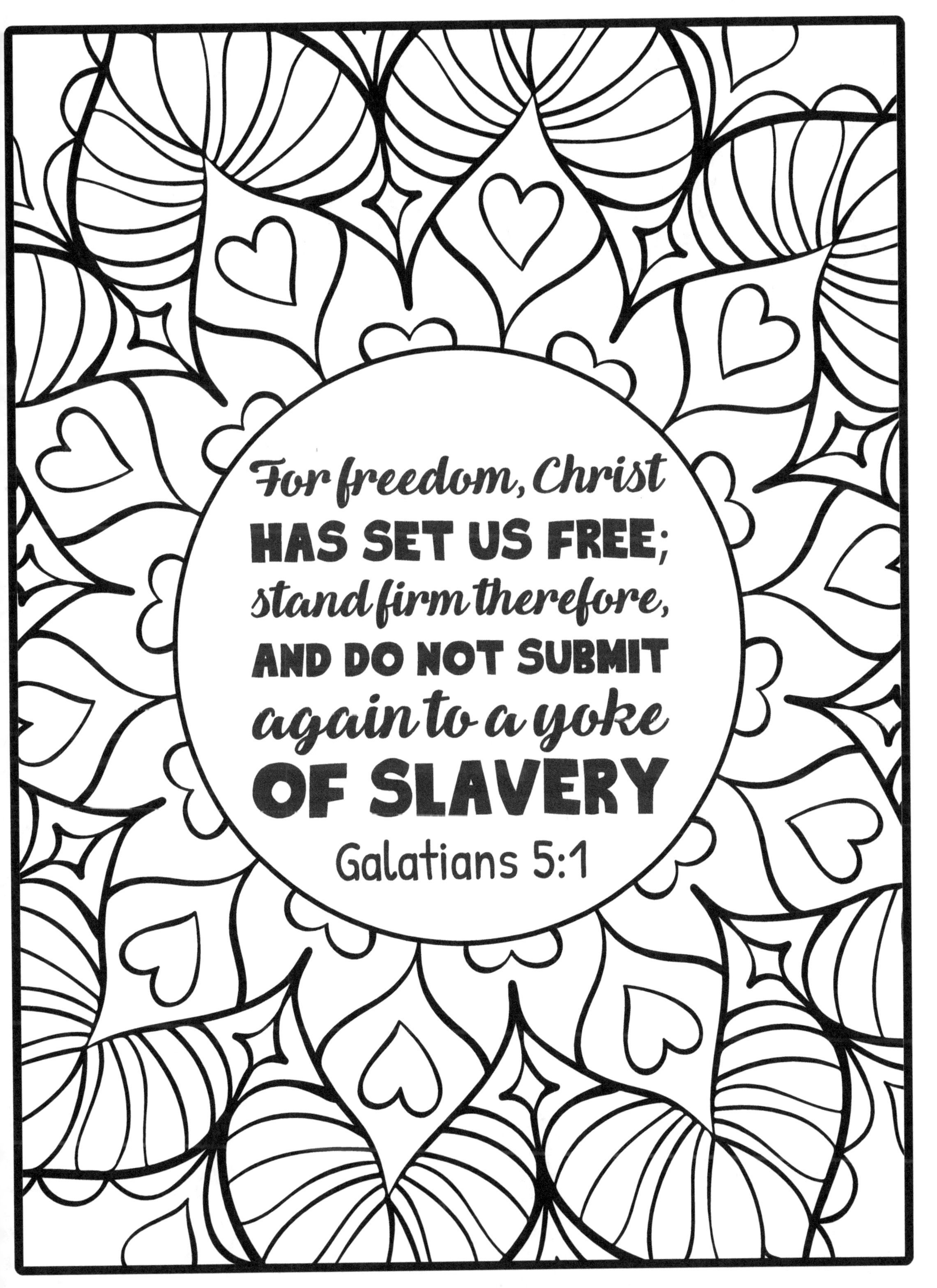

For freedom, Christ
HAS SET US FREE;
stand firm therefore,
AND DO NOT SUBMIT
again to a yoke
OF SLAVERY
Galatians 5:1

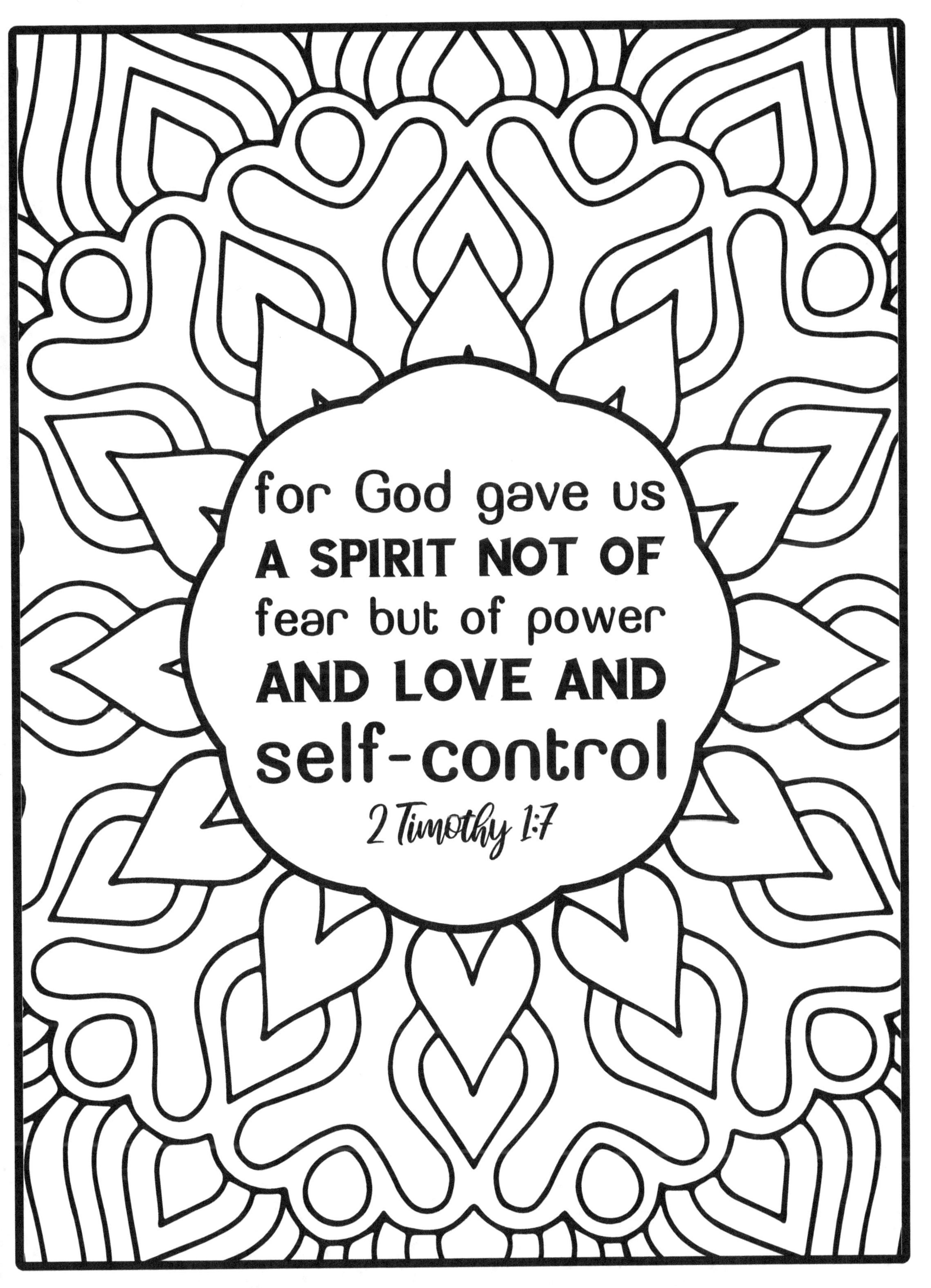

for God gave us
A SPIRIT NOT OF
fear but of power
AND LOVE AND
self-control
2 Timothy 1:7

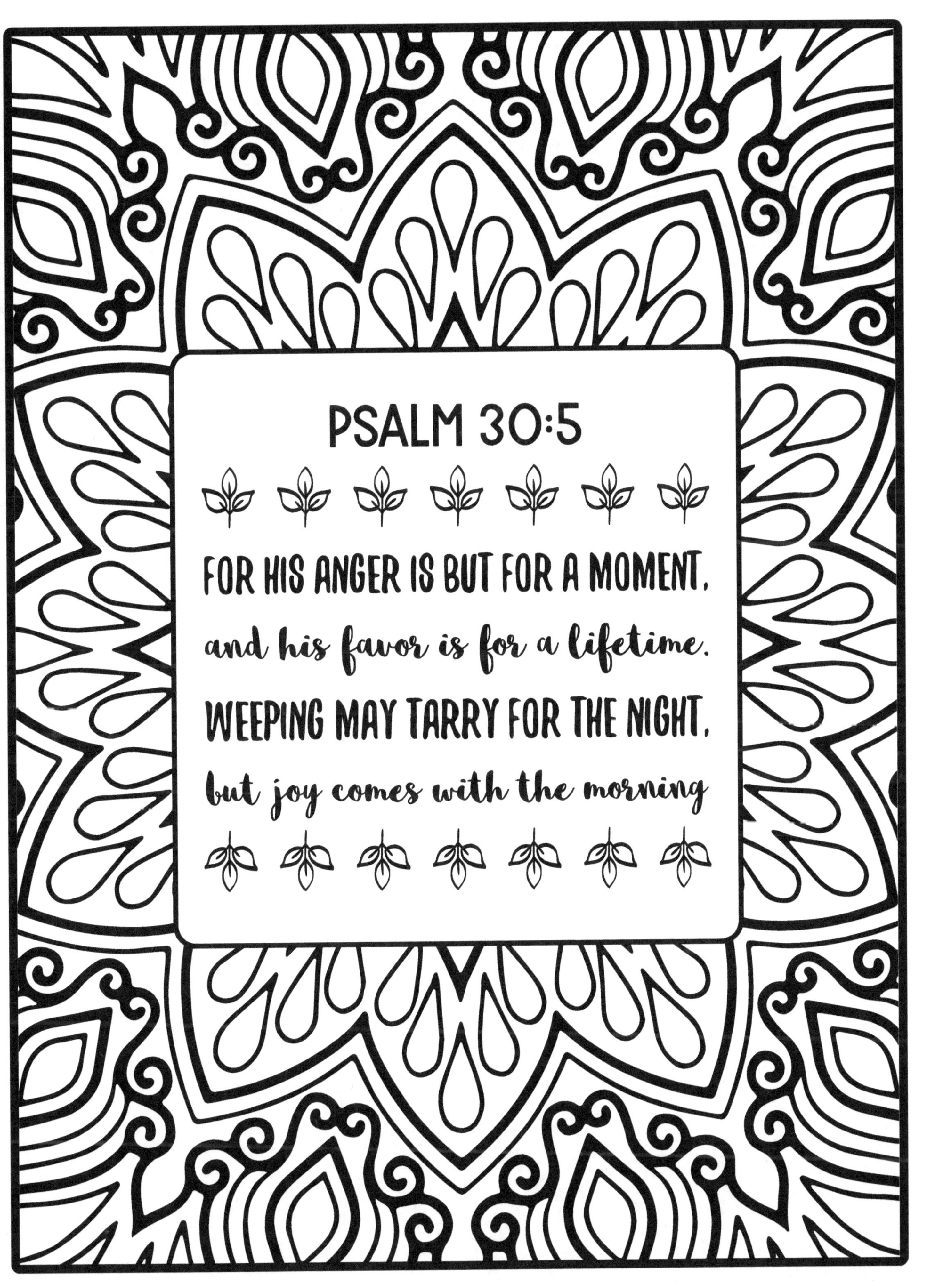

PSALM 30:5

FOR HIS ANGER IS BUT FOR A MOMENT,
and his favor is for a lifetime.
WEEPING MAY TARRY FOR THE NIGHT,
but joy comes with the morning

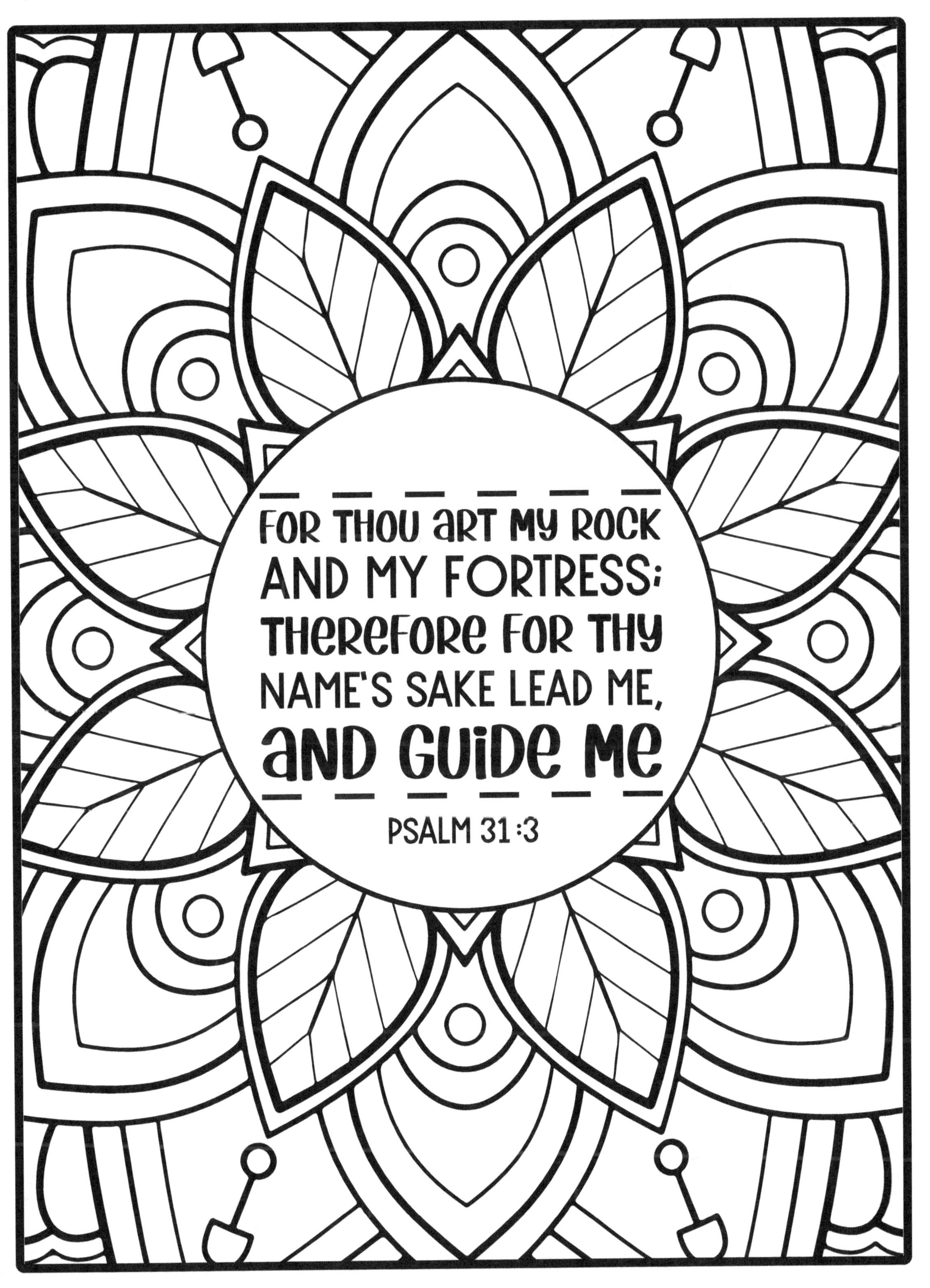

FOR THOU ART MY ROCK AND MY FORTRESS; THEREFORE FOR THY NAME'S SAKE LEAD ME, AND GUIDE ME
PSALM 31:3

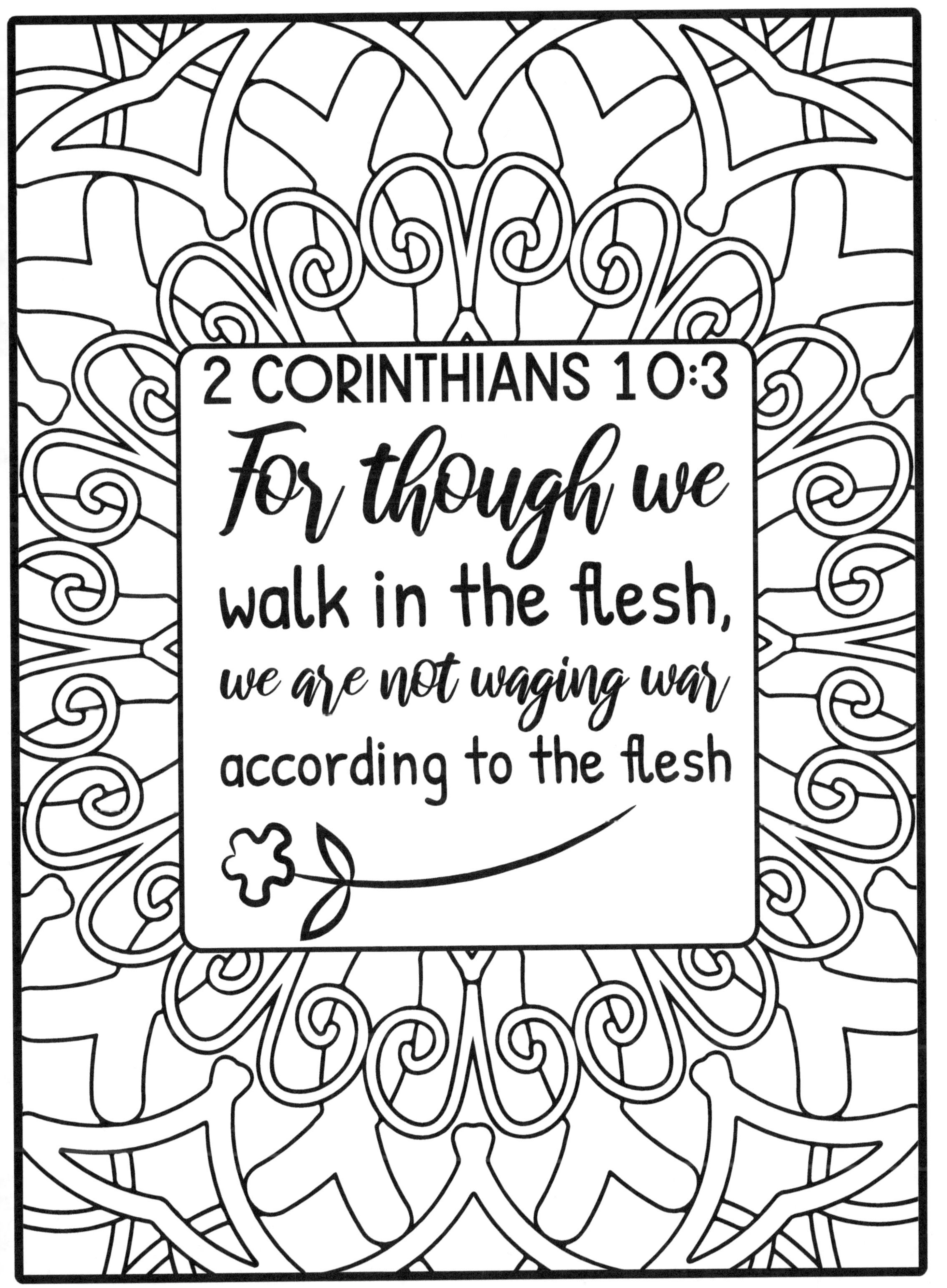

2 CORINTHIANS 10:3
For though we walk in the flesh, we are not waging war according to the flesh

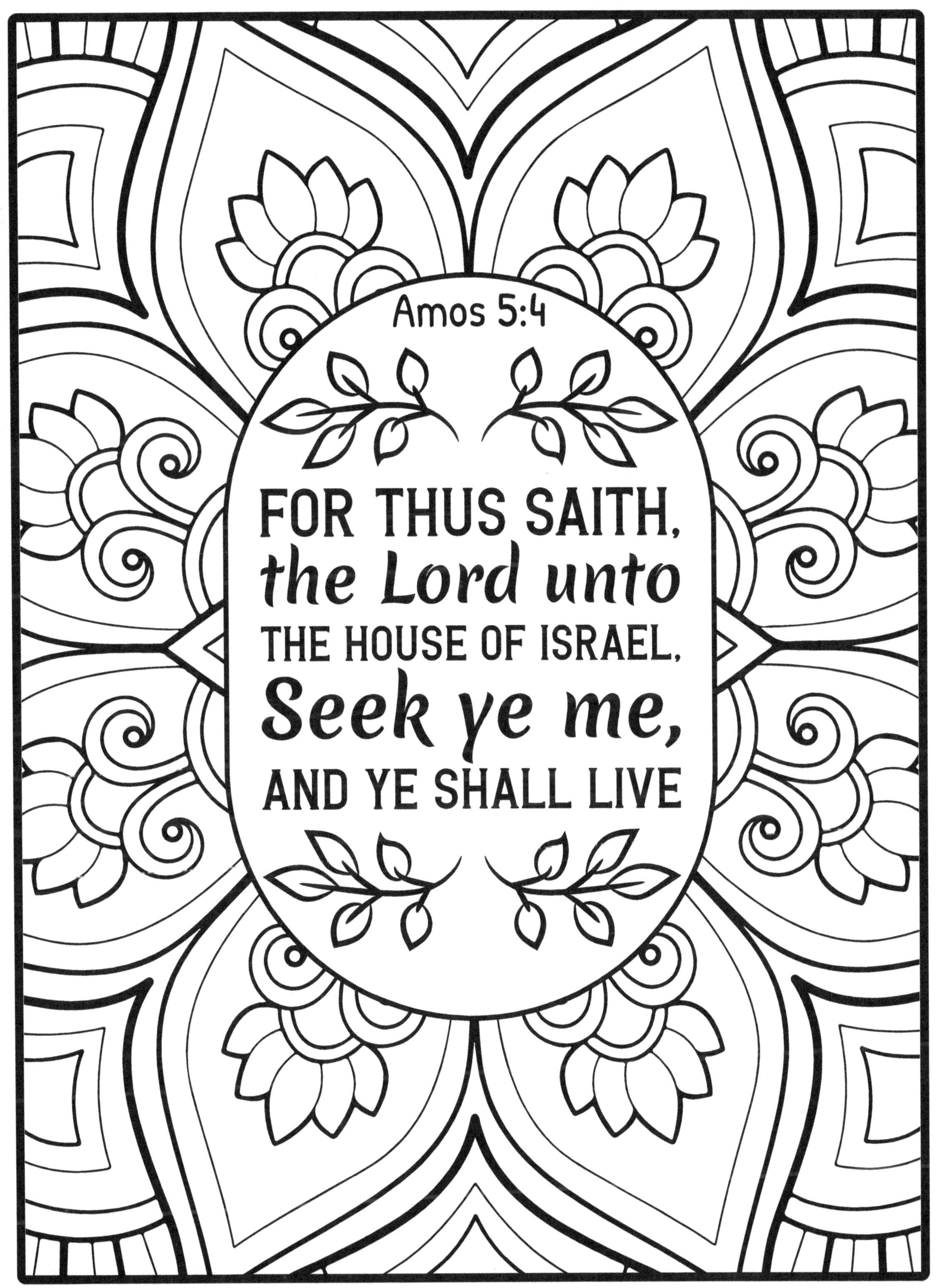

Amos 5:4
FOR THUS SAITH,
the Lord unto
THE HOUSE OF ISRAEL,
Seek ye me,
AND YE SHALL LIVE

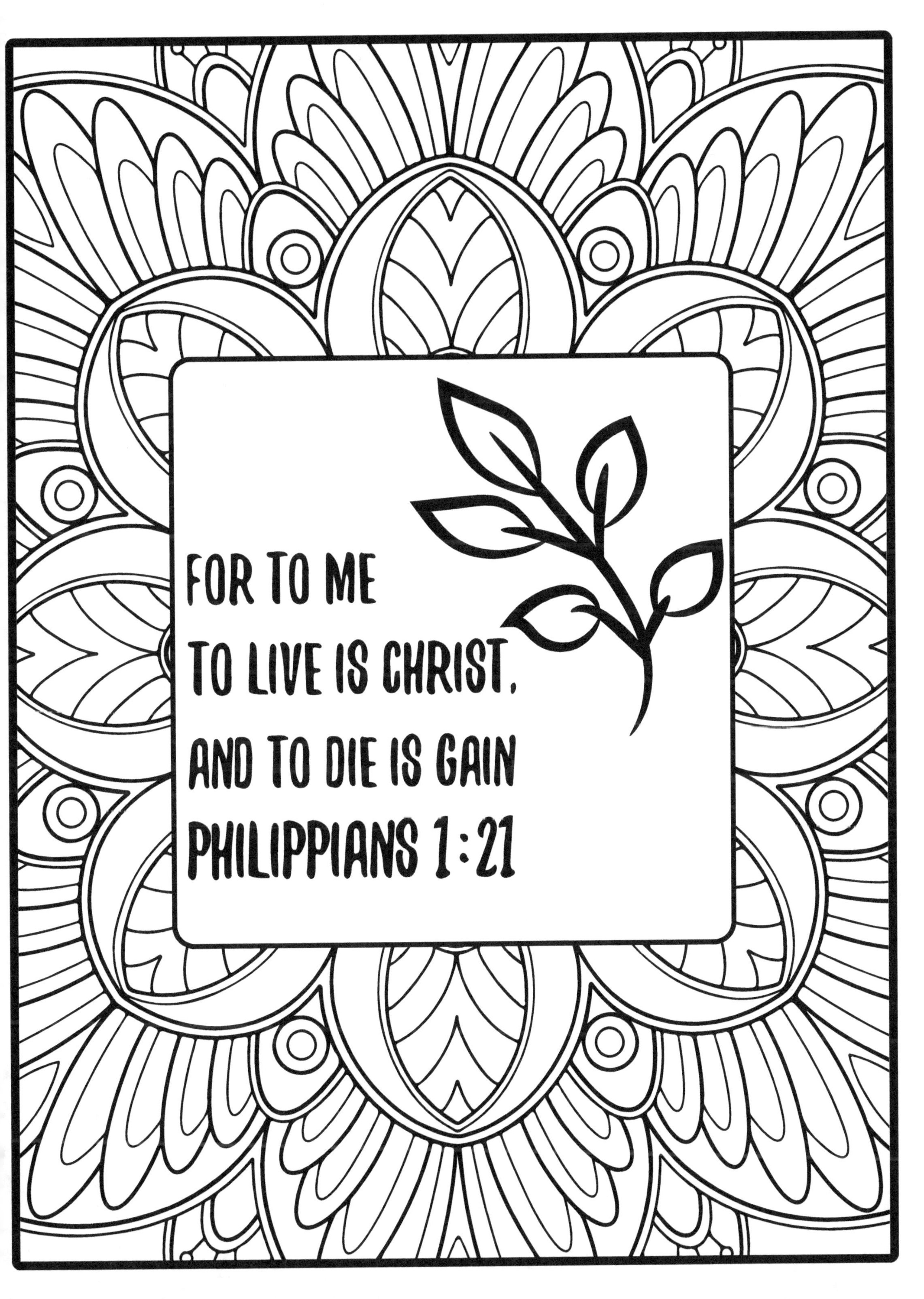

FOR TO ME
TO LIVE IS CHRIST,
AND TO DIE IS GAIN
PHILIPPIANS 1:21

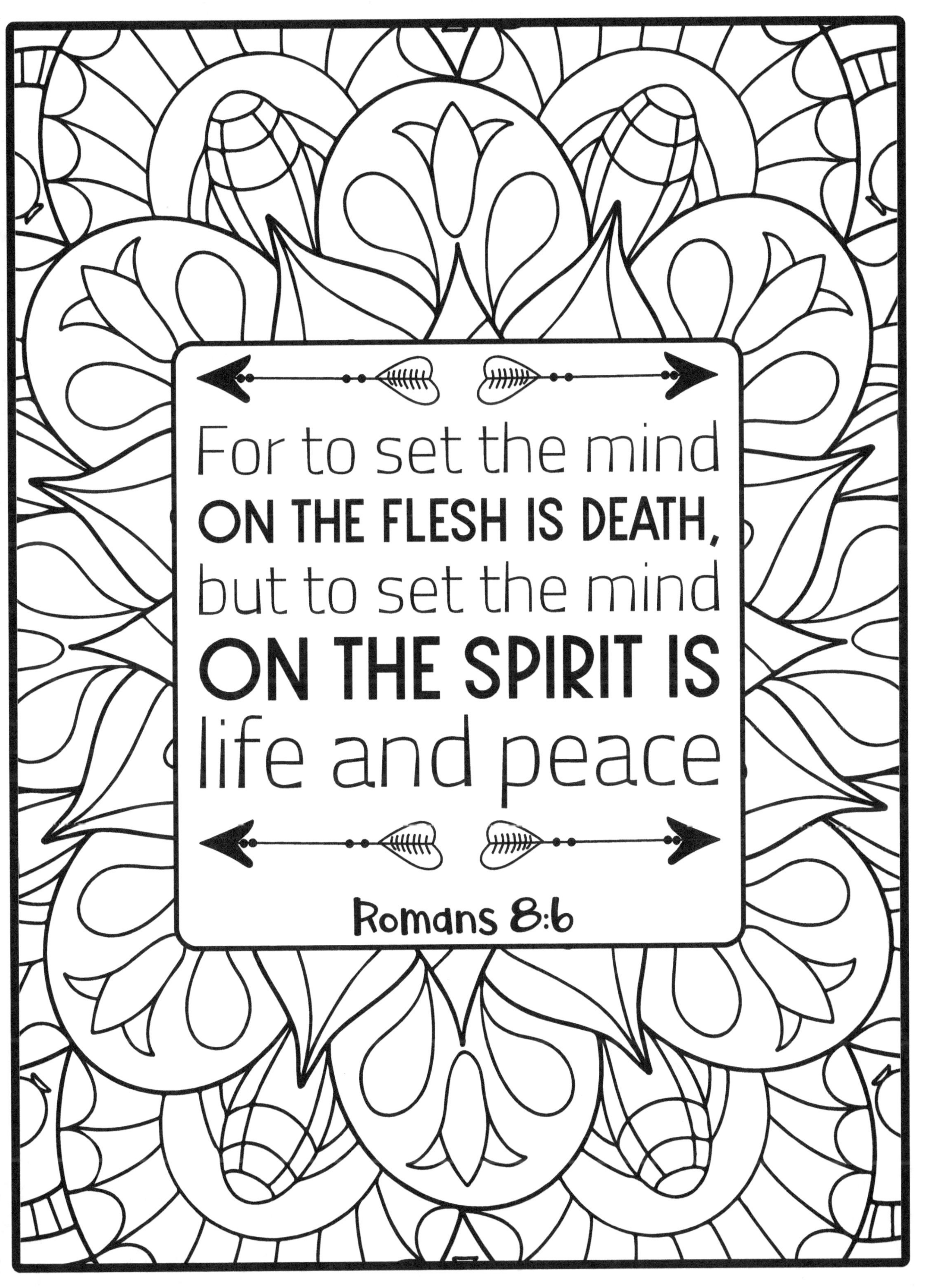

For to set the mind ON THE FLESH IS DEATH, but to set the mind ON THE SPIRIT IS life and peace
Romans 8:6

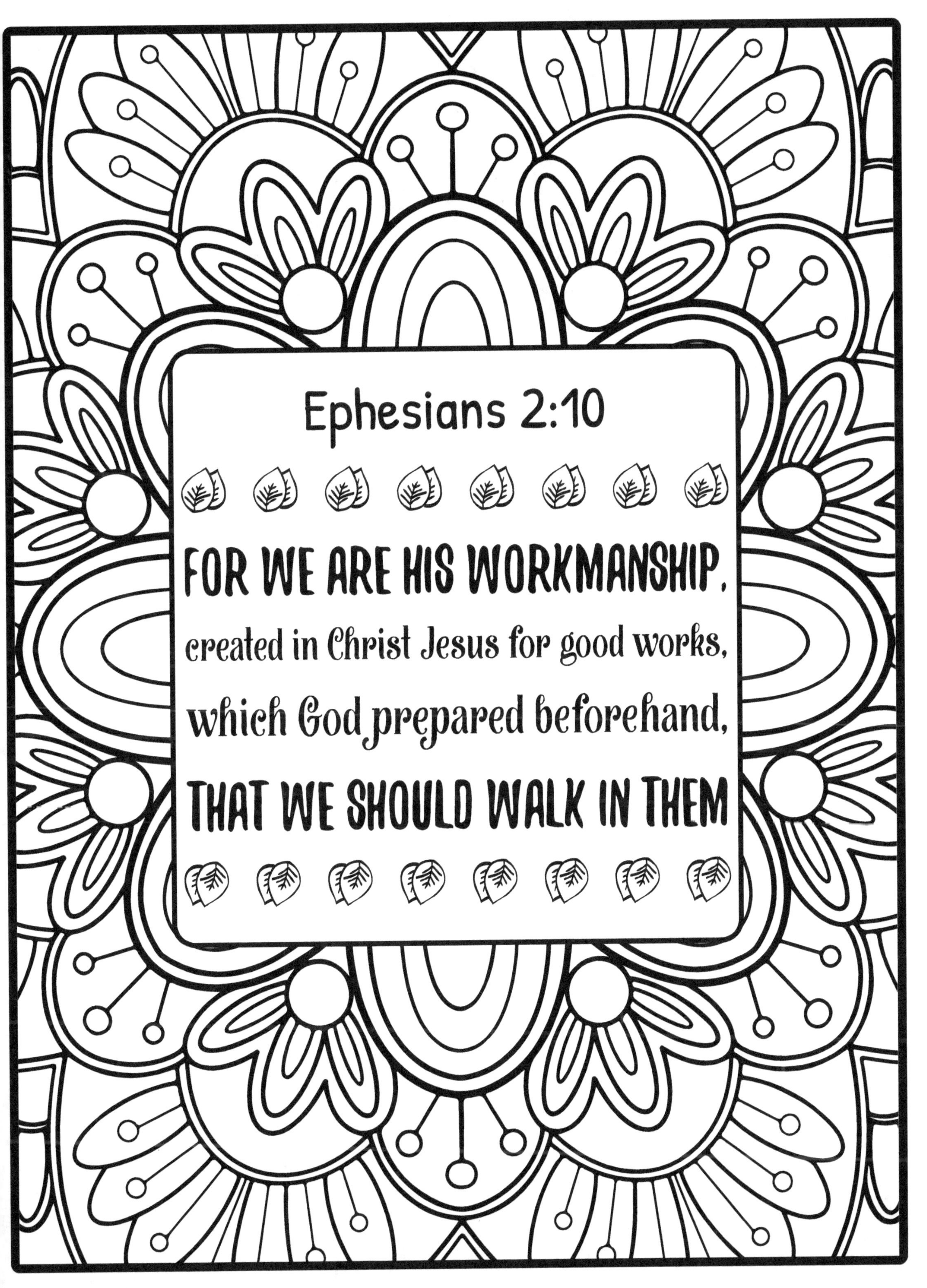

Ephesians 2:10
FOR WE ARE HIS WORKMANSHIP,
created in Christ Jesus for good works,
which God prepared beforehand,
THAT WE SHOULD WALK IN THEM

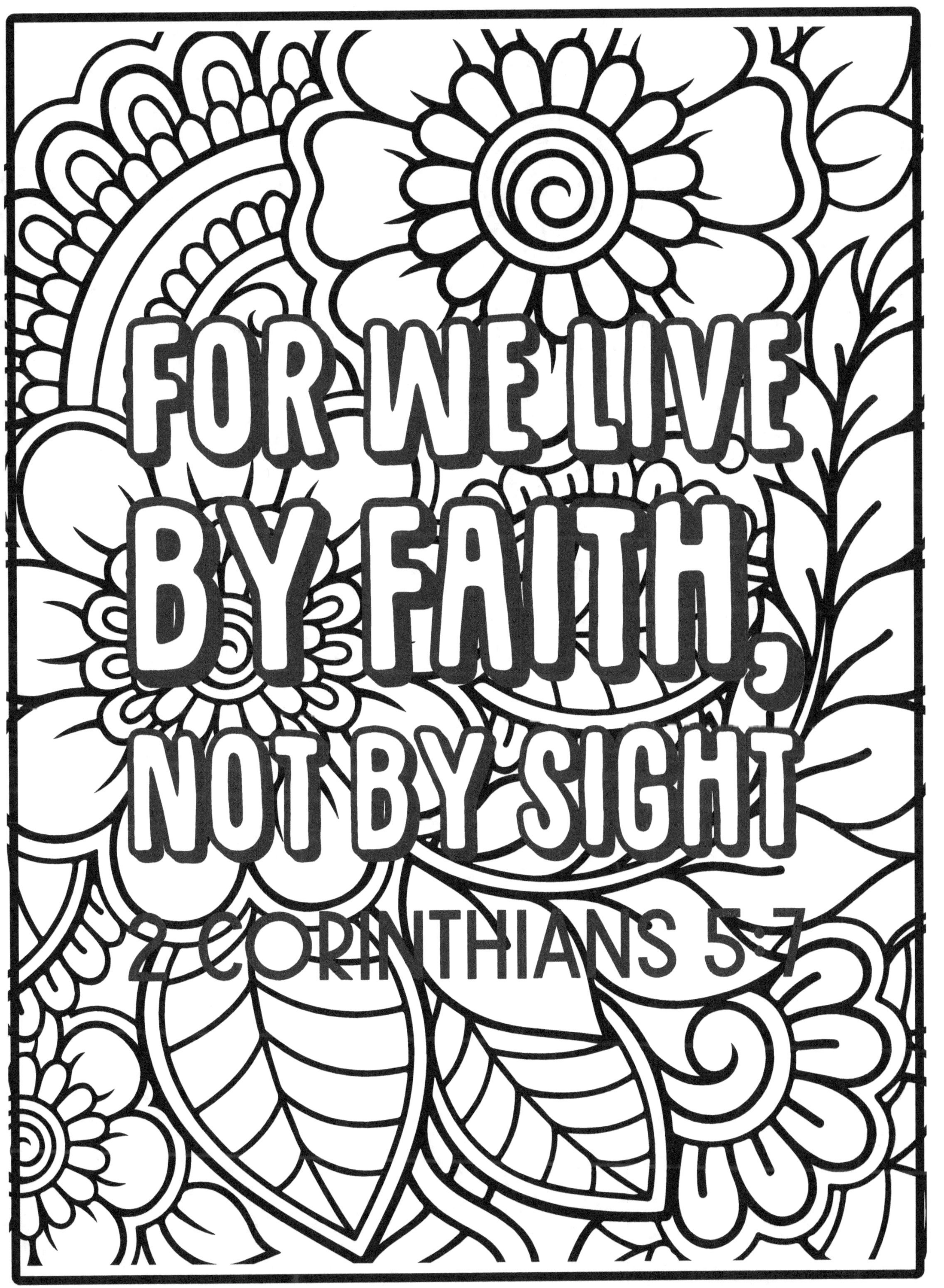FOR WE LIVE
BY FAITH,
NOT BY SIGHT
2 CORINTHIANS 5:7

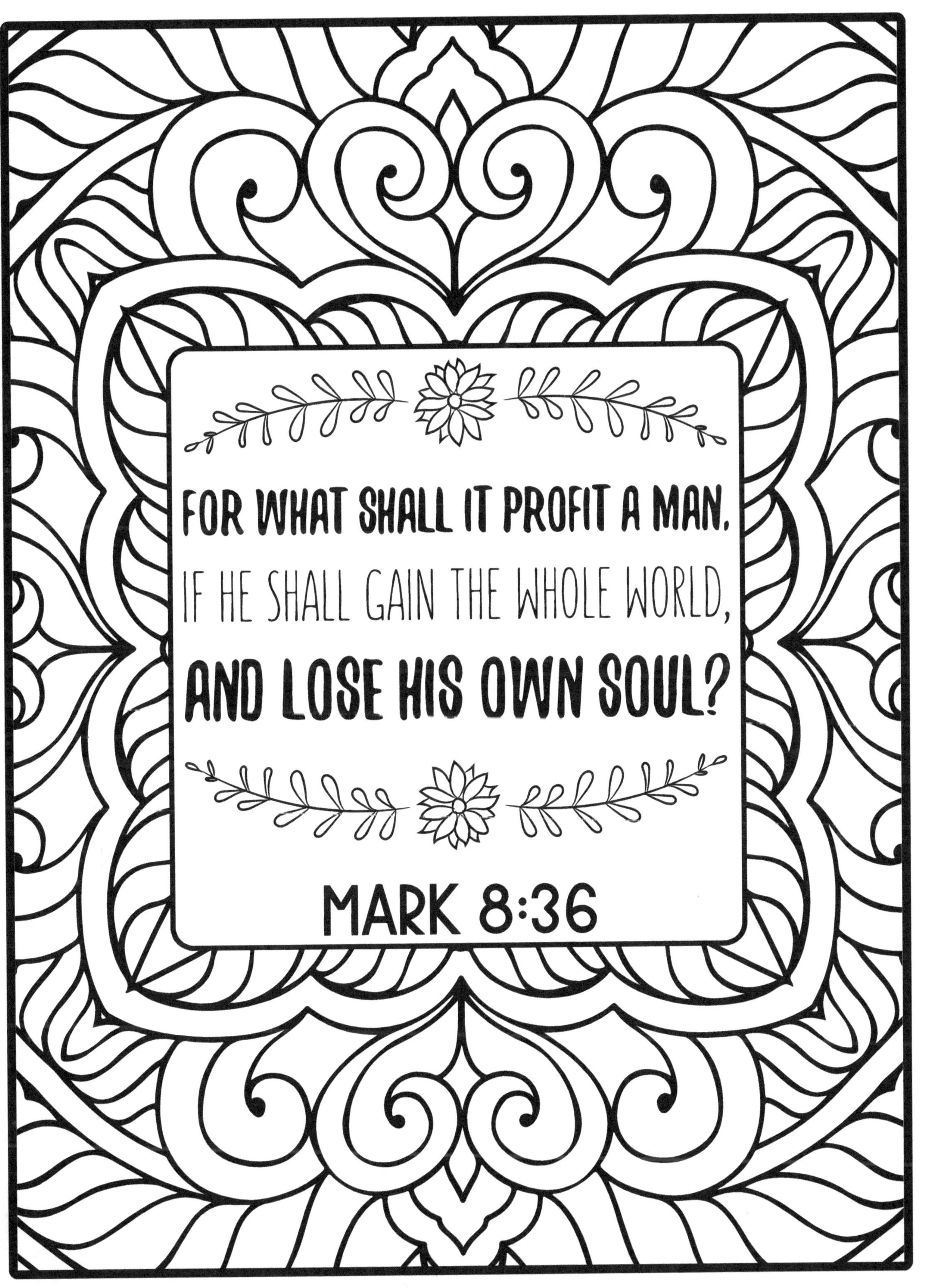

FOR WHAT SHALL IT PROFIT A MAN,
IF HE SHALL GAIN THE WHOLE WORLD,
AND LOSE HIS OWN SOUL?
MARK 8:36

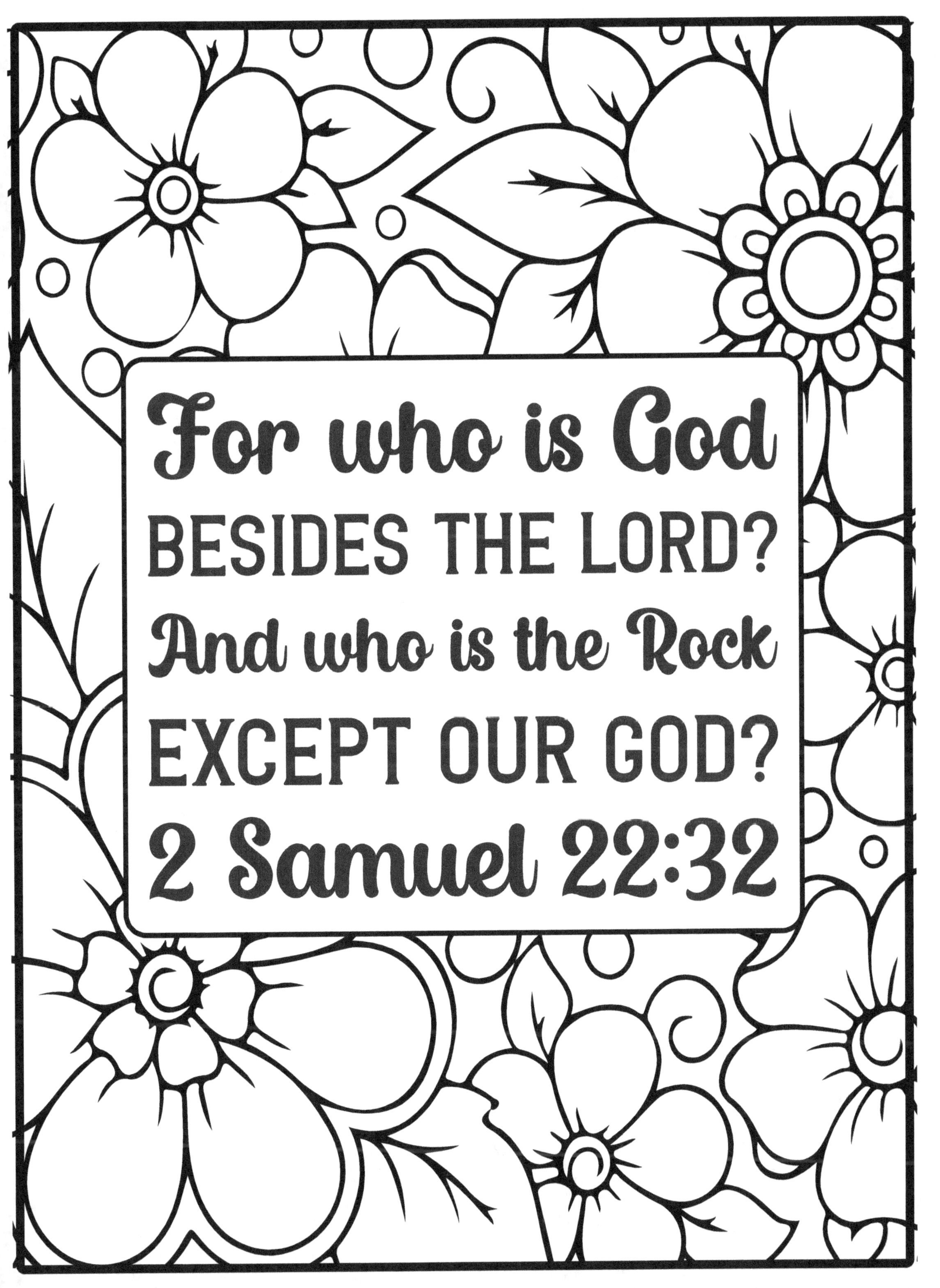

For who is God BESIDES THE LORD? And who is the Rock EXCEPT OUR GOD?
2 Samuel 22:32

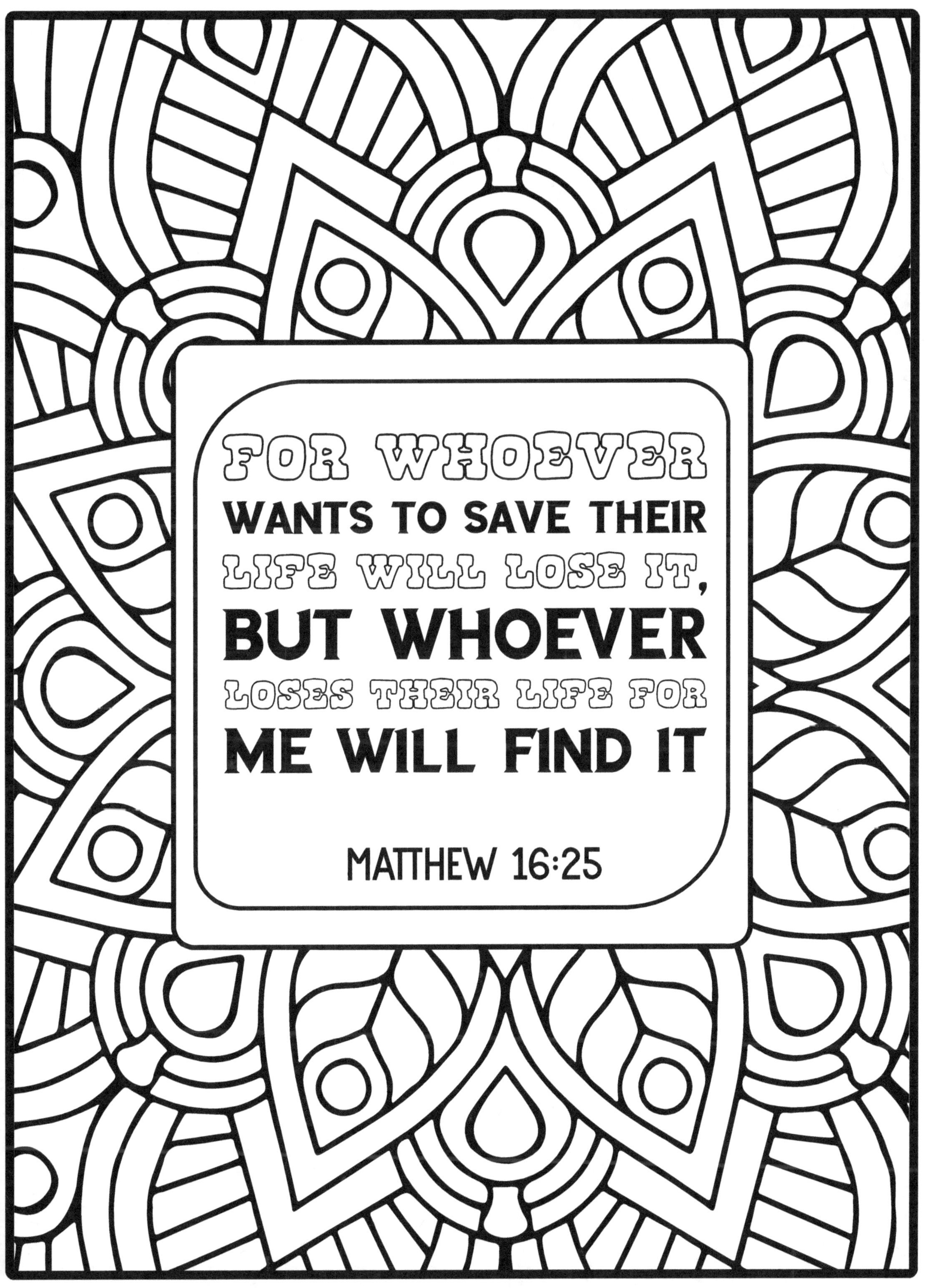
FOR WHOEVER
WANTS TO SAVE THEIR
LIFE WILL LOSE IT,
BUT WHOEVER
LOSES THEIR LIFE FOR
ME WILL FIND IT

MATTHEW 16:25

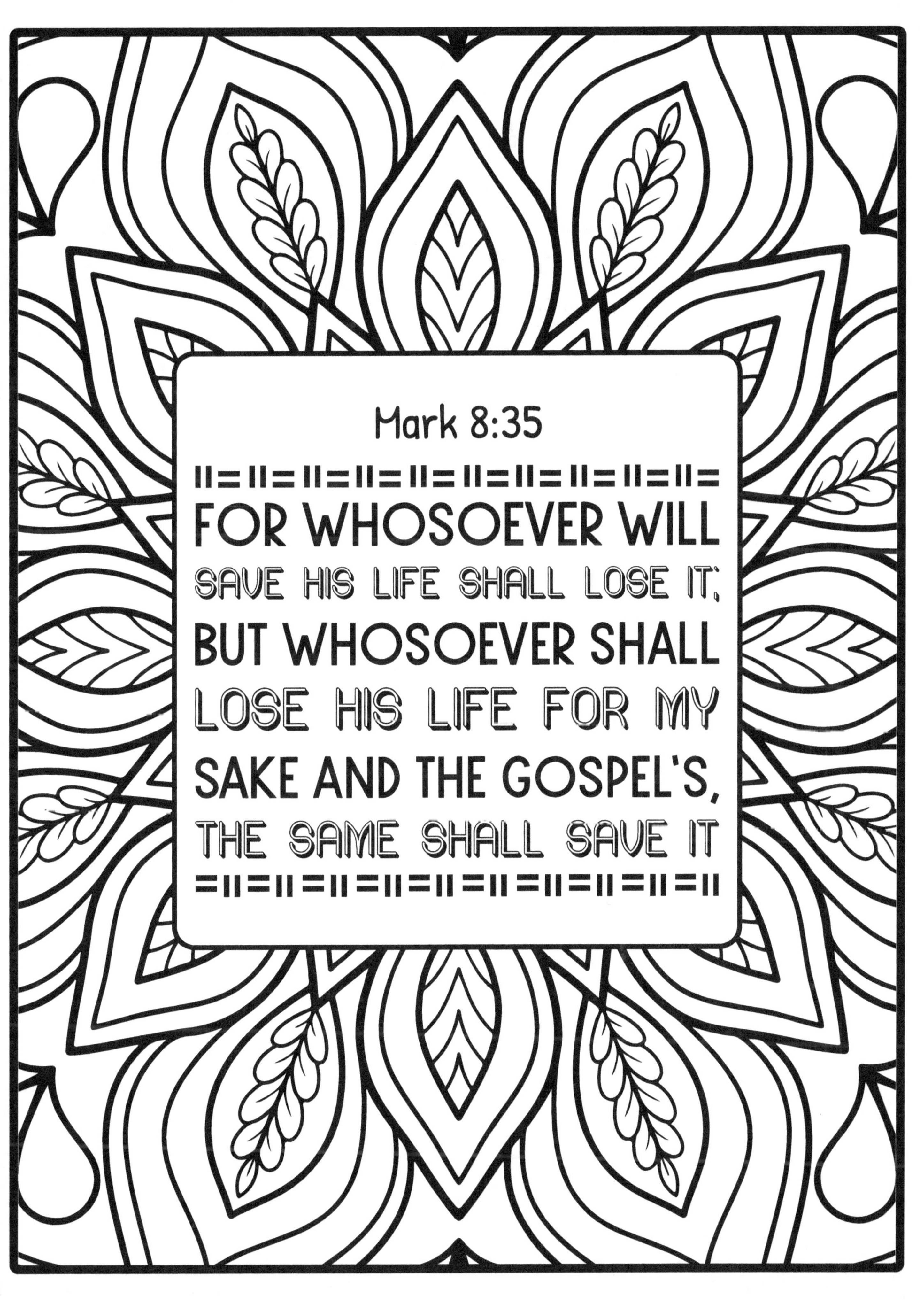

Mark 8:35
FOR WHOSOEVER WILL SAVE HIS LIFE SHALL LOSE IT; BUT WHOSOEVER SHALL LOSE HIS LIFE FOR MY SAKE AND THE GOSPEL'S, THE SAME SHALL SAVE IT

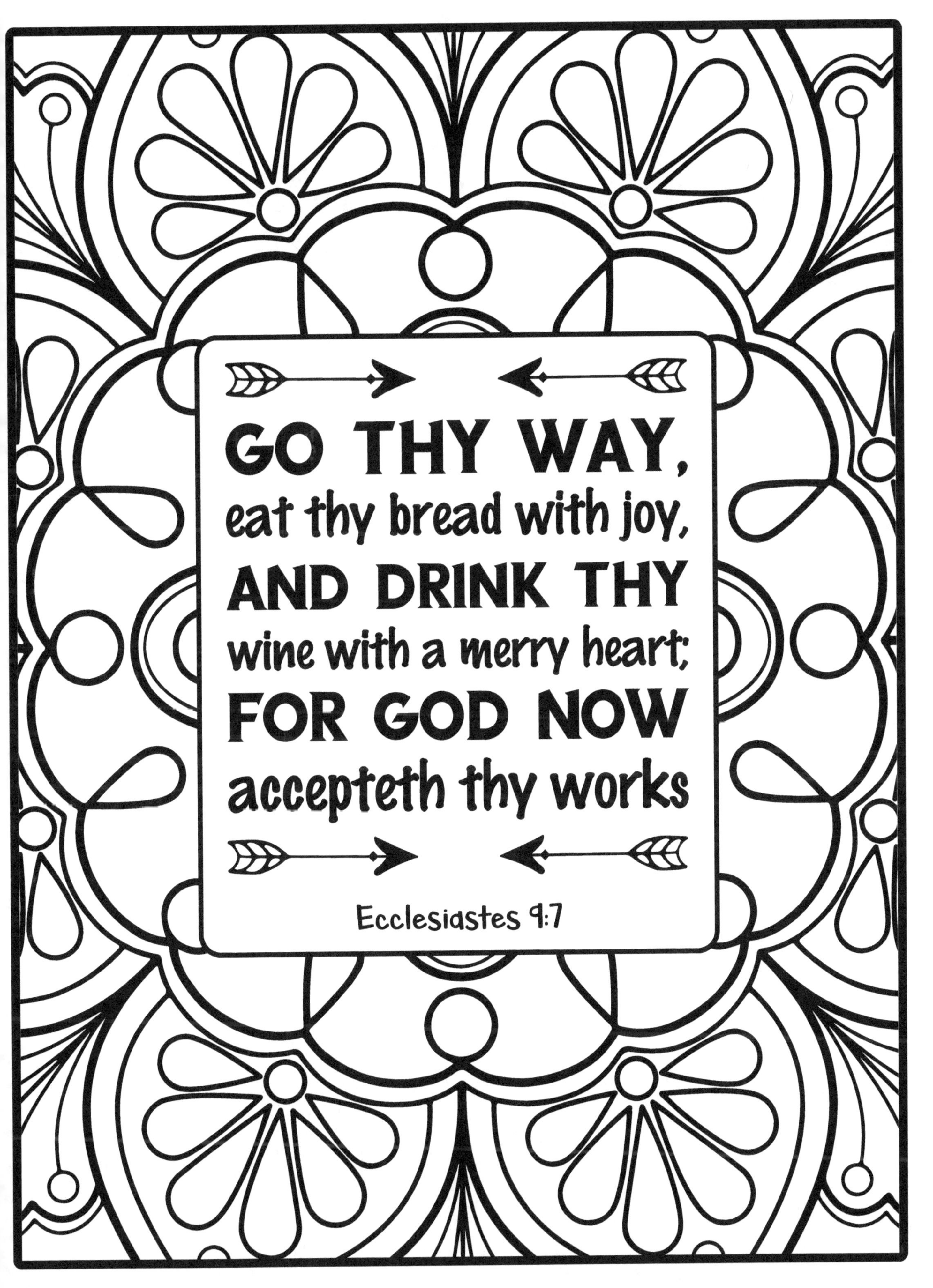

GO THY WAY,
eat thy bread with joy,
AND DRINK THY
wine with a merry heart;
FOR GOD NOW
accepteth thy works
Ecclesiastes 9:7

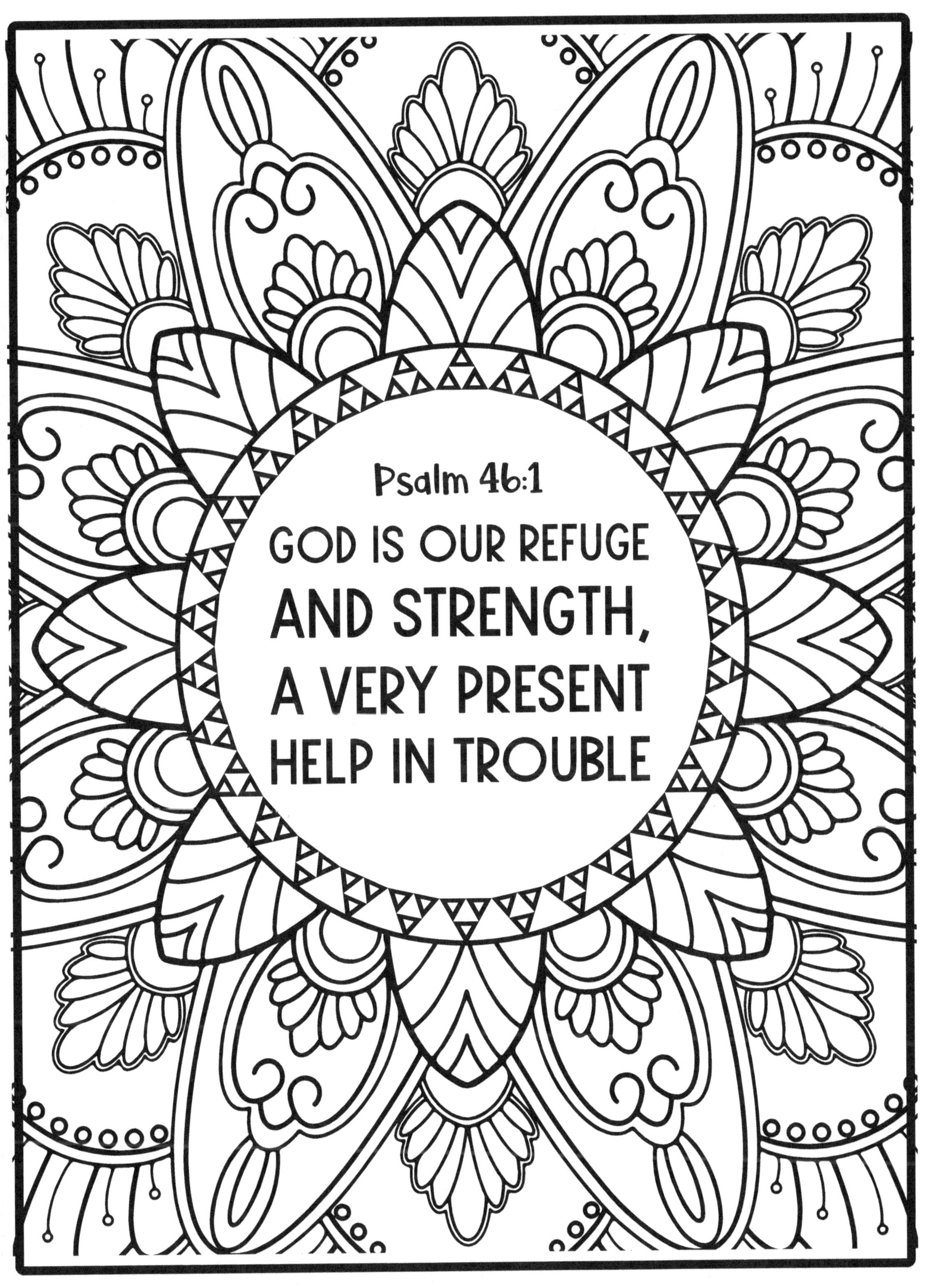

Psalm 46:1
GOD IS OUR REFUGE
AND STRENGTH,
A VERY PRESENT
HELP IN TROUBLE

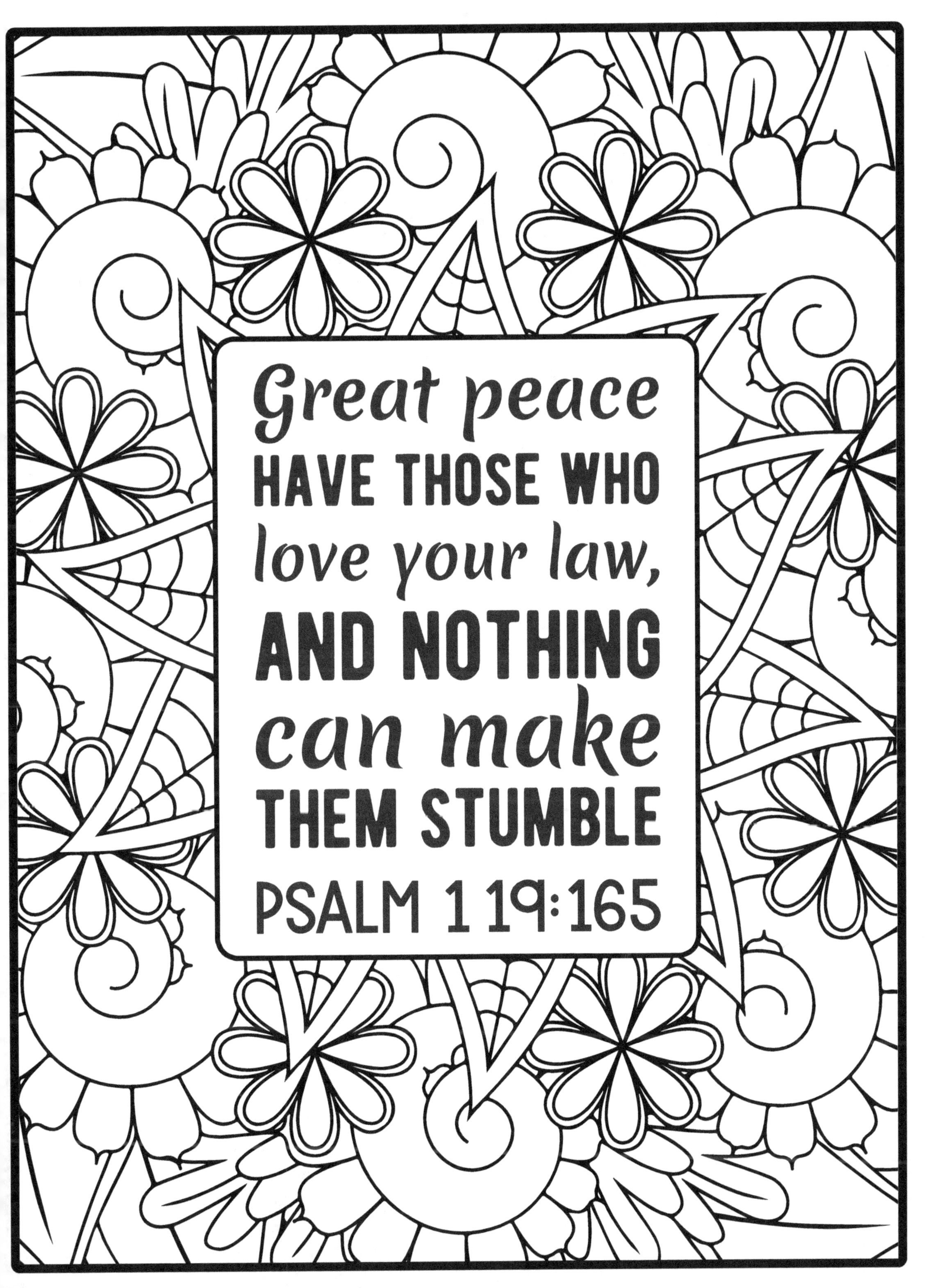

Great peace
HAVE THOSE WHO
love your law,
AND NOTHING
can make
THEM STUMBLE
PSALM 1 19:165

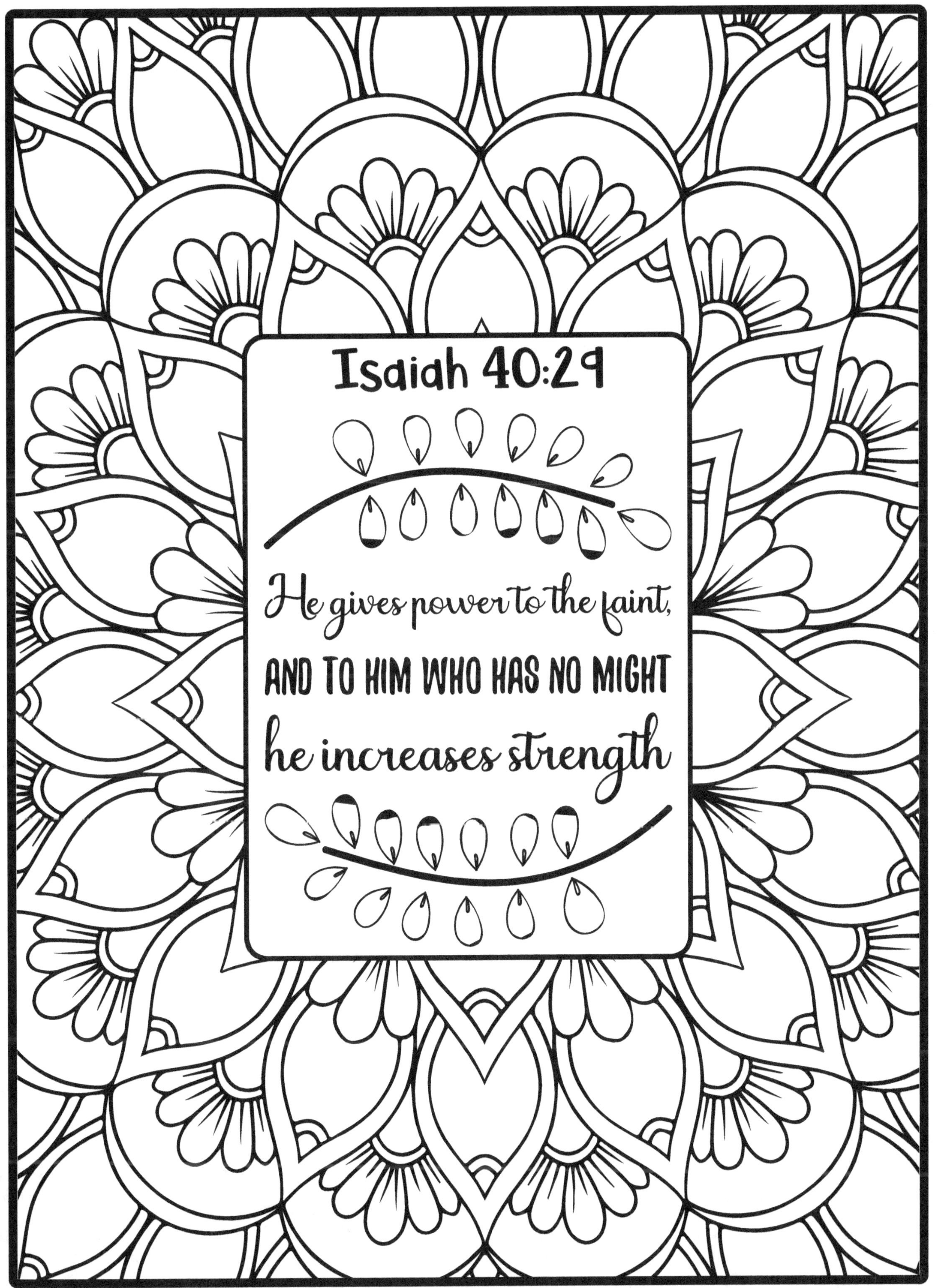

Isaiah 40:29
He gives power to the faint,
AND TO HIM WHO HAS NO MIGHT
he increases strength

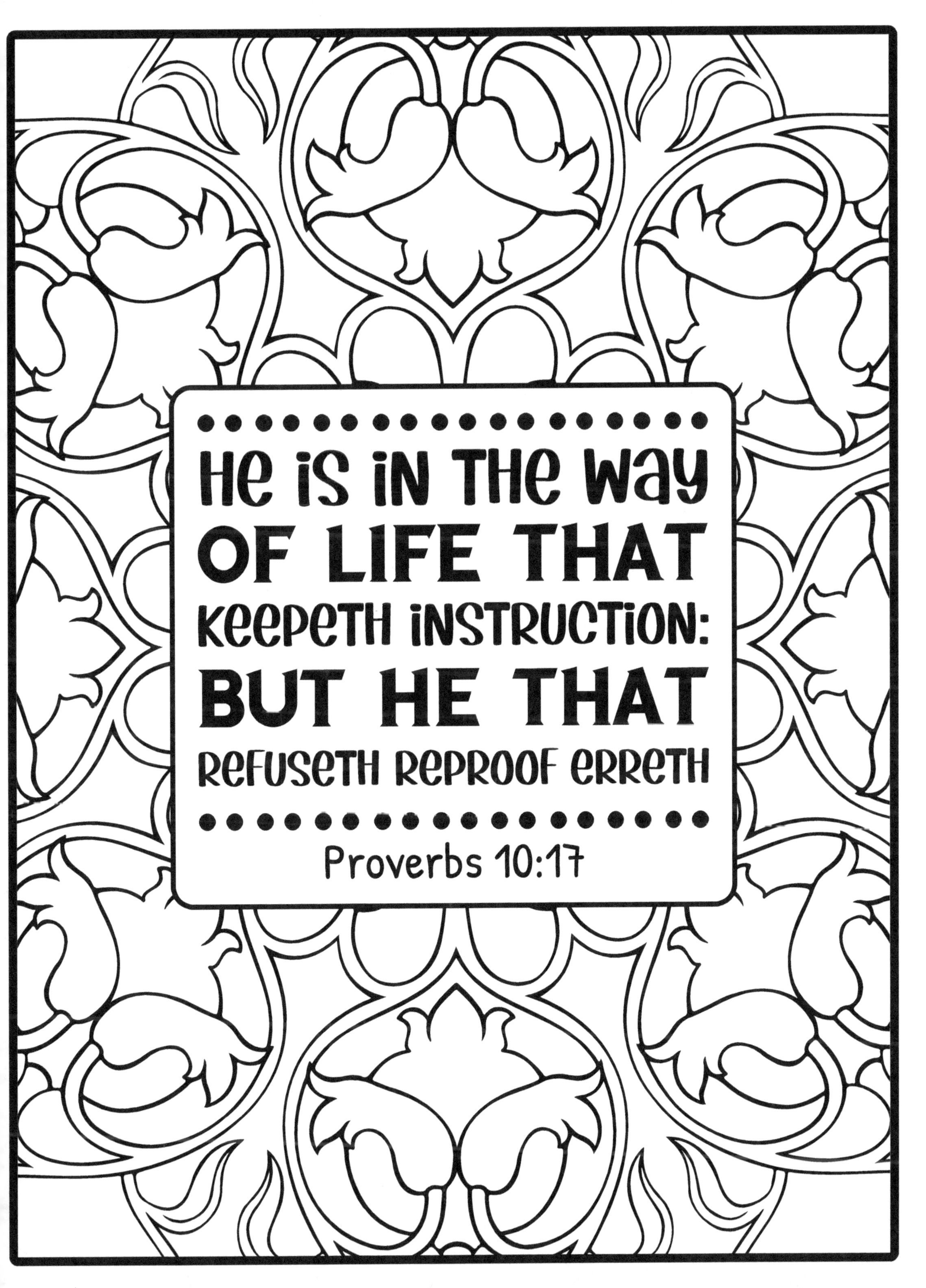

He is in the way
of life that
keepeth instruction:
but he that
refuseth reproof erreth
Proverbs 10:17

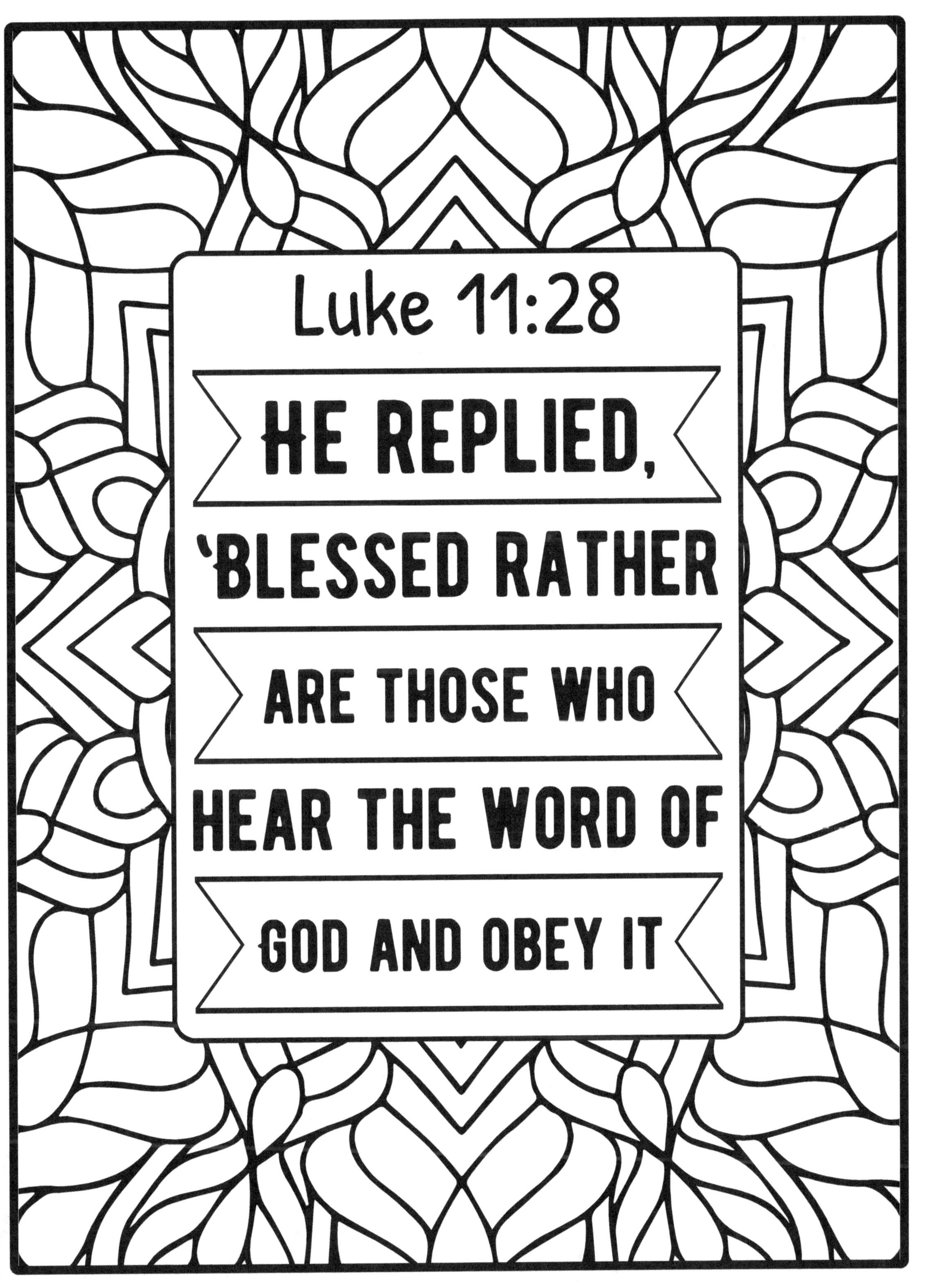

Luke 11:28
HE REPLIED,
'BLESSED RATHER
ARE THOSE WHO
HEAR THE WORD OF
GOD AND OBEY IT

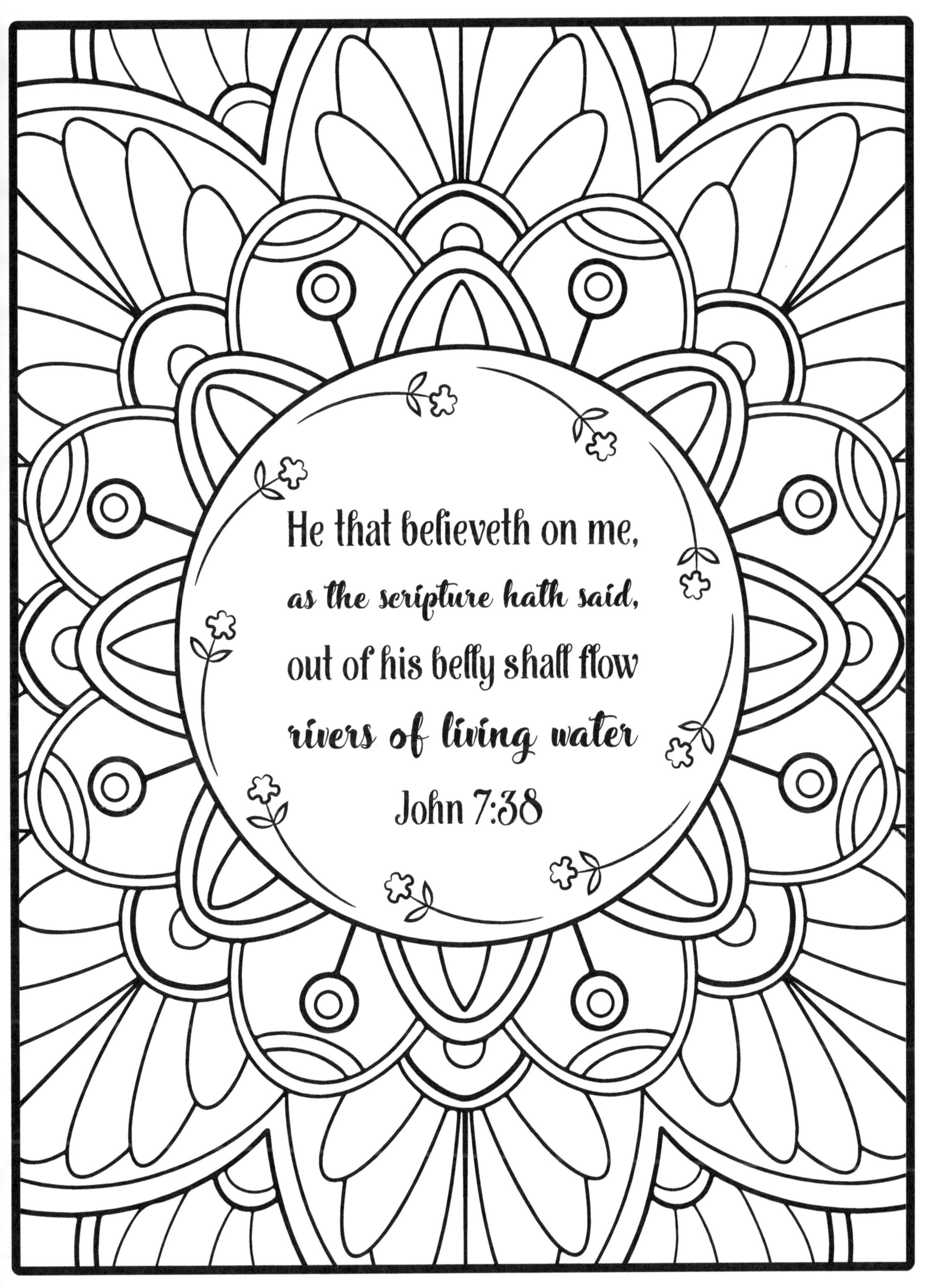
He that believeth on me,
as the scripture hath said,
out of his belly shall flow
rivers of living water
John 7:38

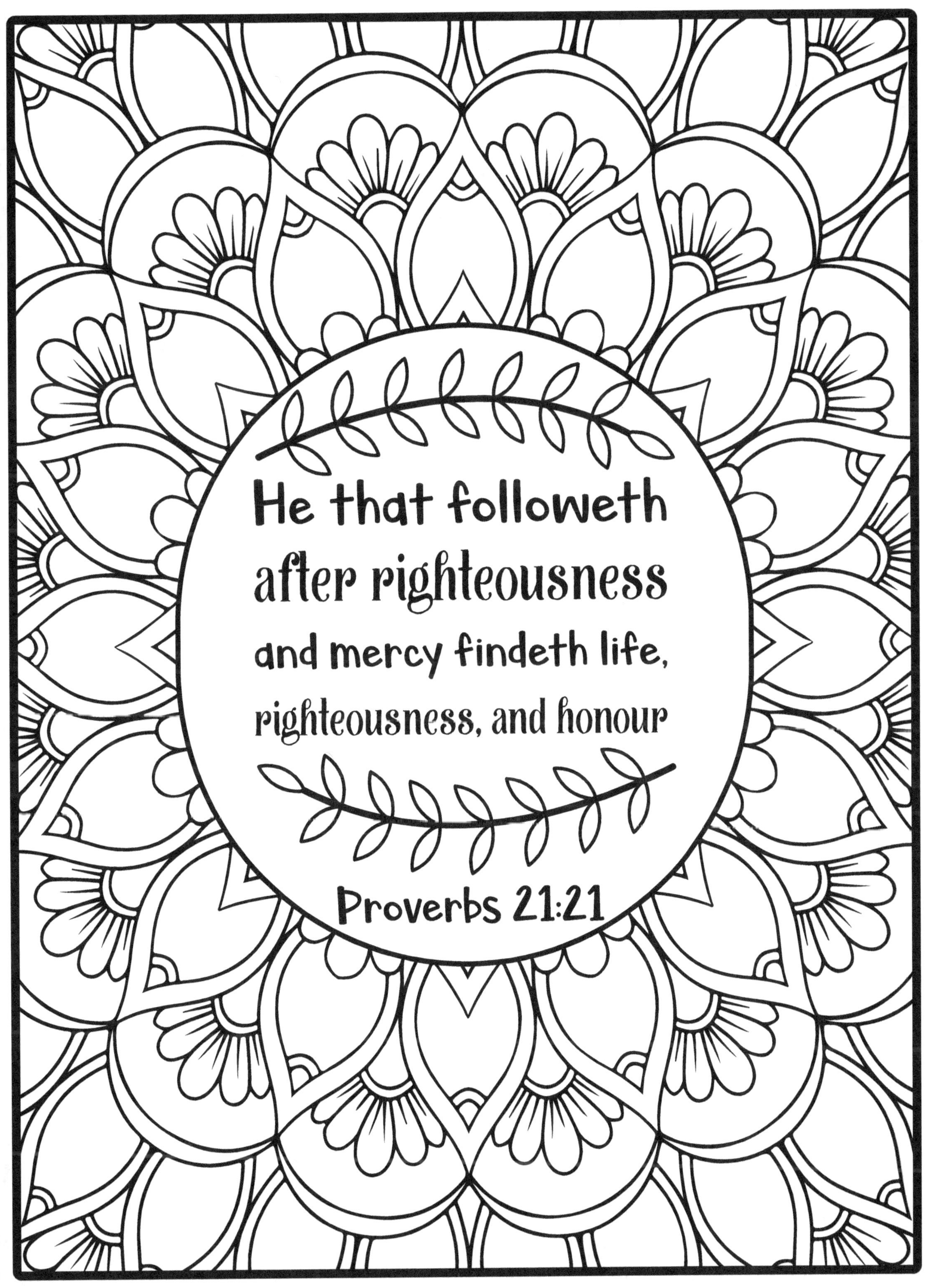
He that followeth
after righteousness
and mercy findeth life,
righteousness, and honour

Proverbs 21:21

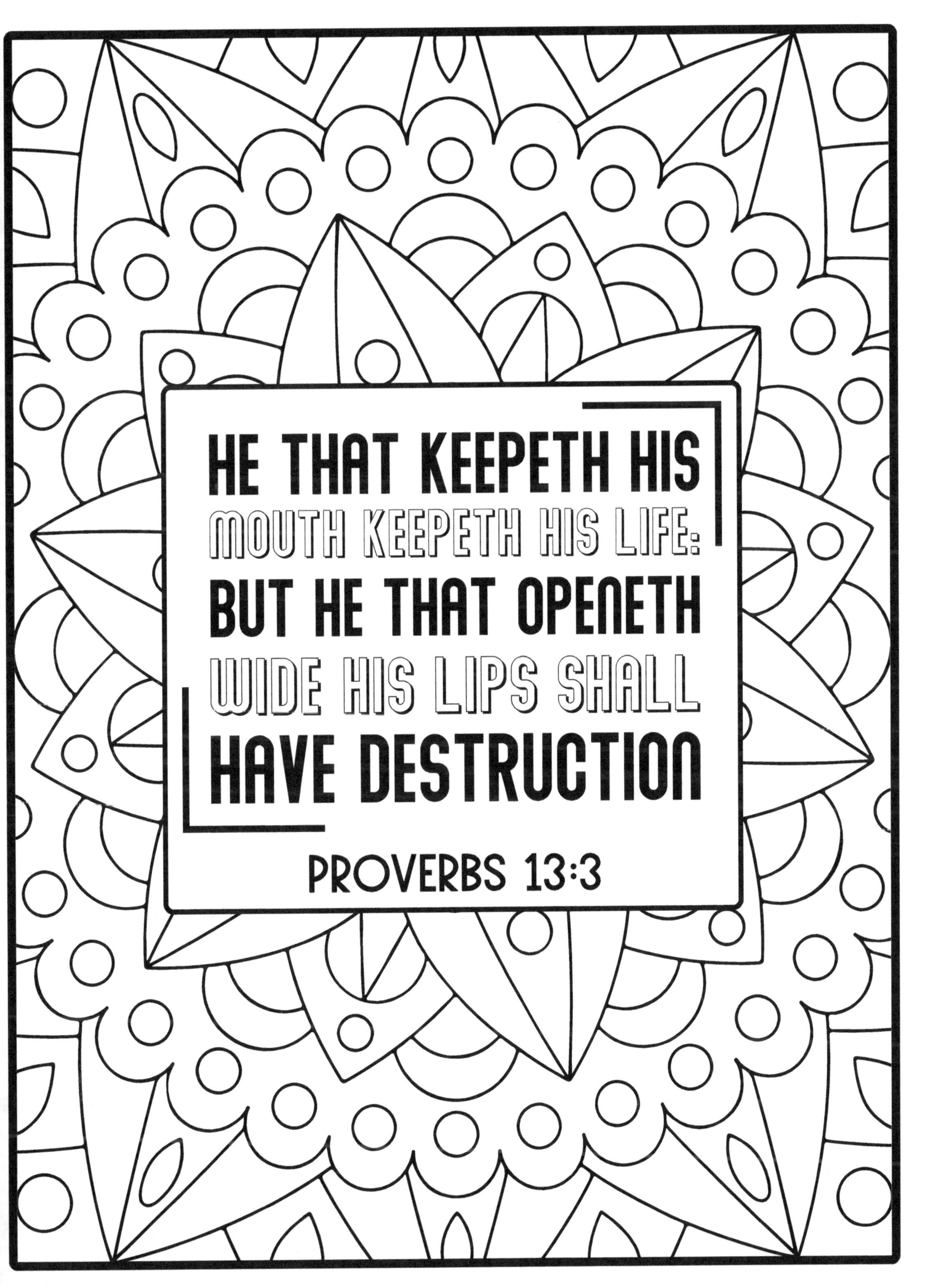

HE THAT KEEPETH HIS
MOUTH KEEPETH HIS LIFE:
BUT HE THAT OPENETH
WIDE HIS LIPS SHALL
HAVE DESTRUCTION
PROVERBS 13:3

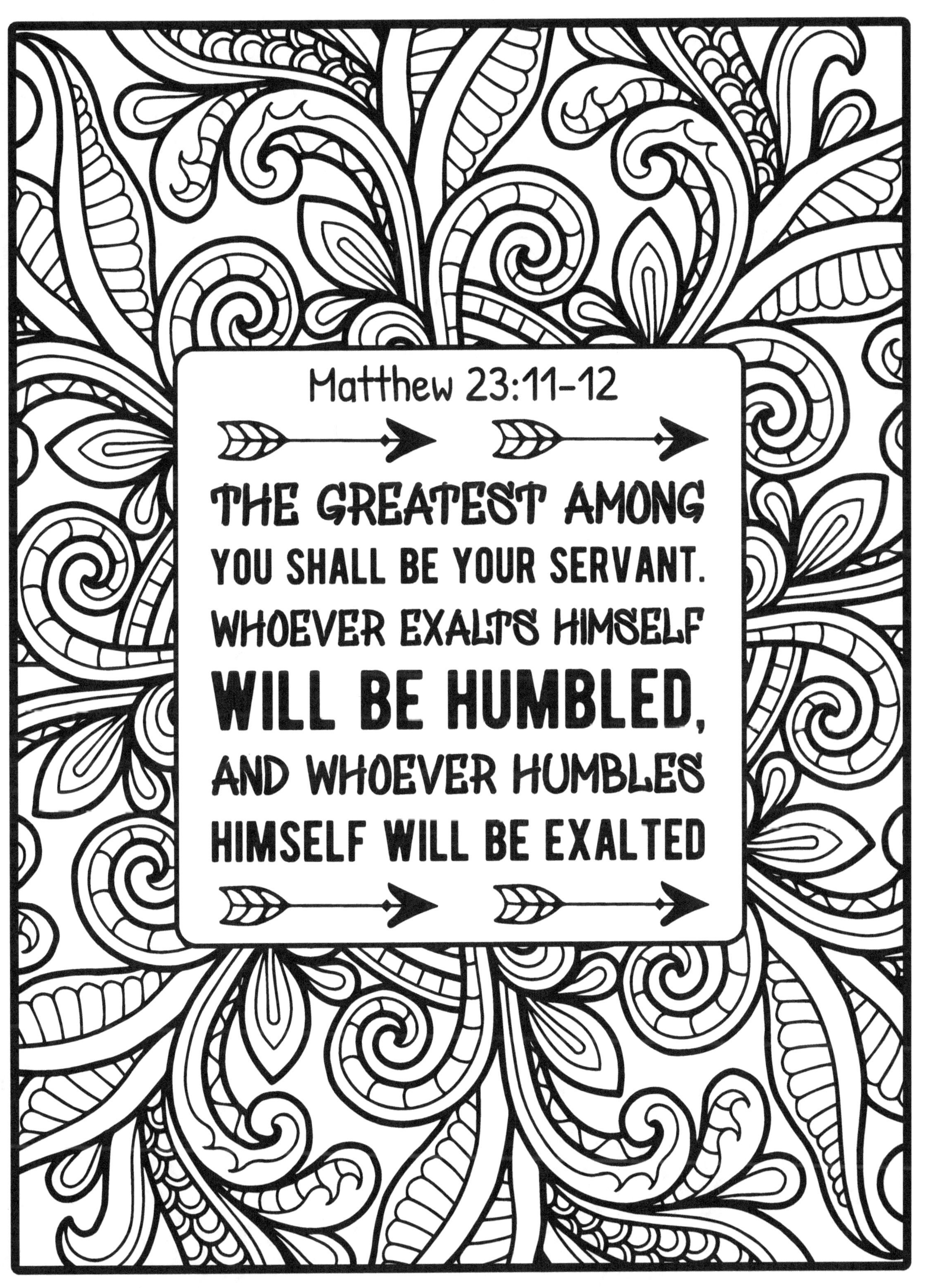

Matthew 23:11-12
THE GREATEST AMONG
YOU SHALL BE YOUR SERVANT.
WHOEVER EXALTS HIMSELF
WILL BE HUMBLED,
AND WHOEVER HUMBLES
HIMSELF WILL BE EXALTED

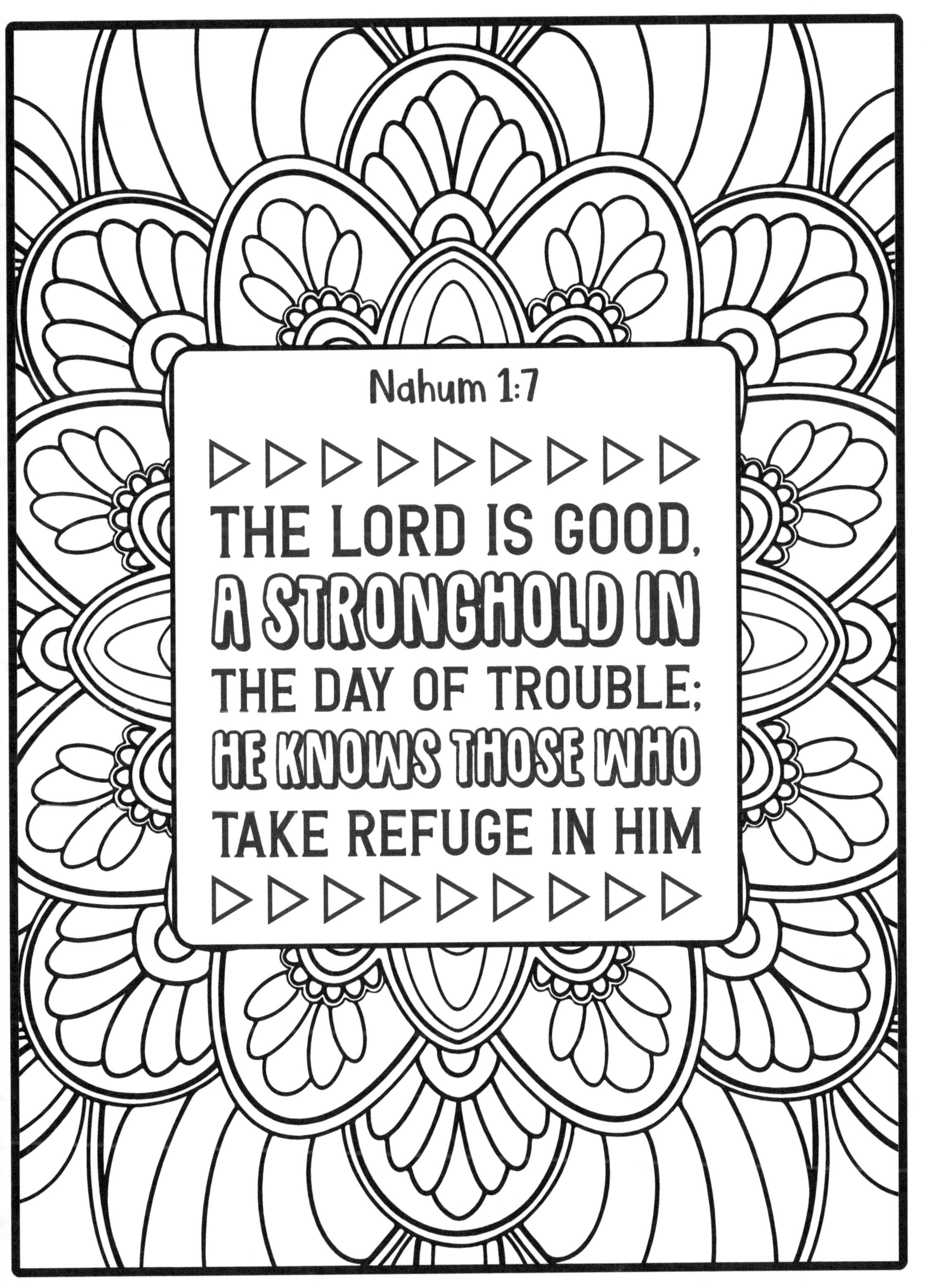

Nahum 1:7
THE LORD IS GOOD,
A STRONGHOLD IN
THE DAY OF TROUBLE;
HE KNOWS THOSE WHO
TAKE REFUGE IN HIM

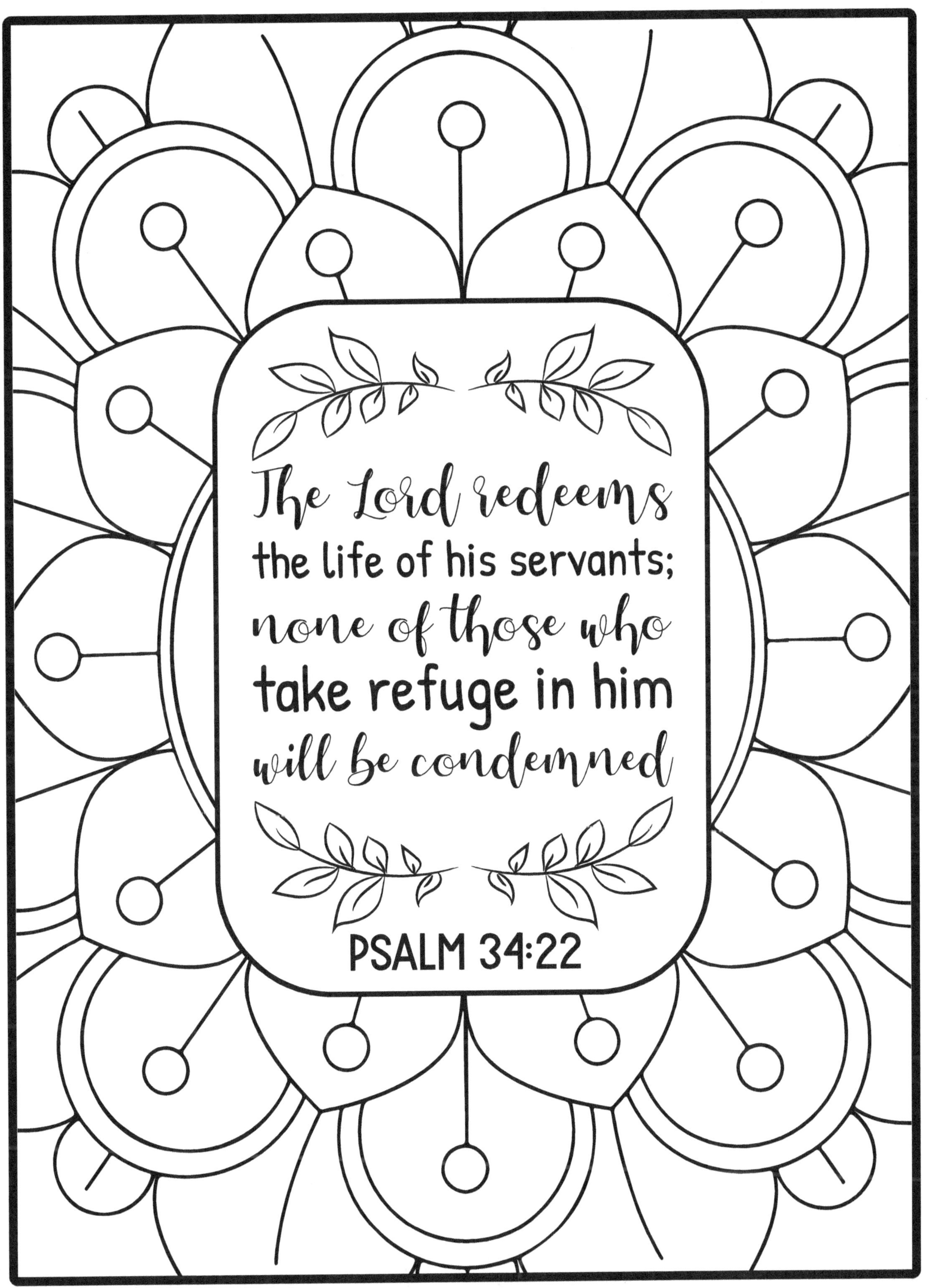

The Lord redeems the life of his servants; none of those who take refuge in him will be condemned

PSALM 34:22

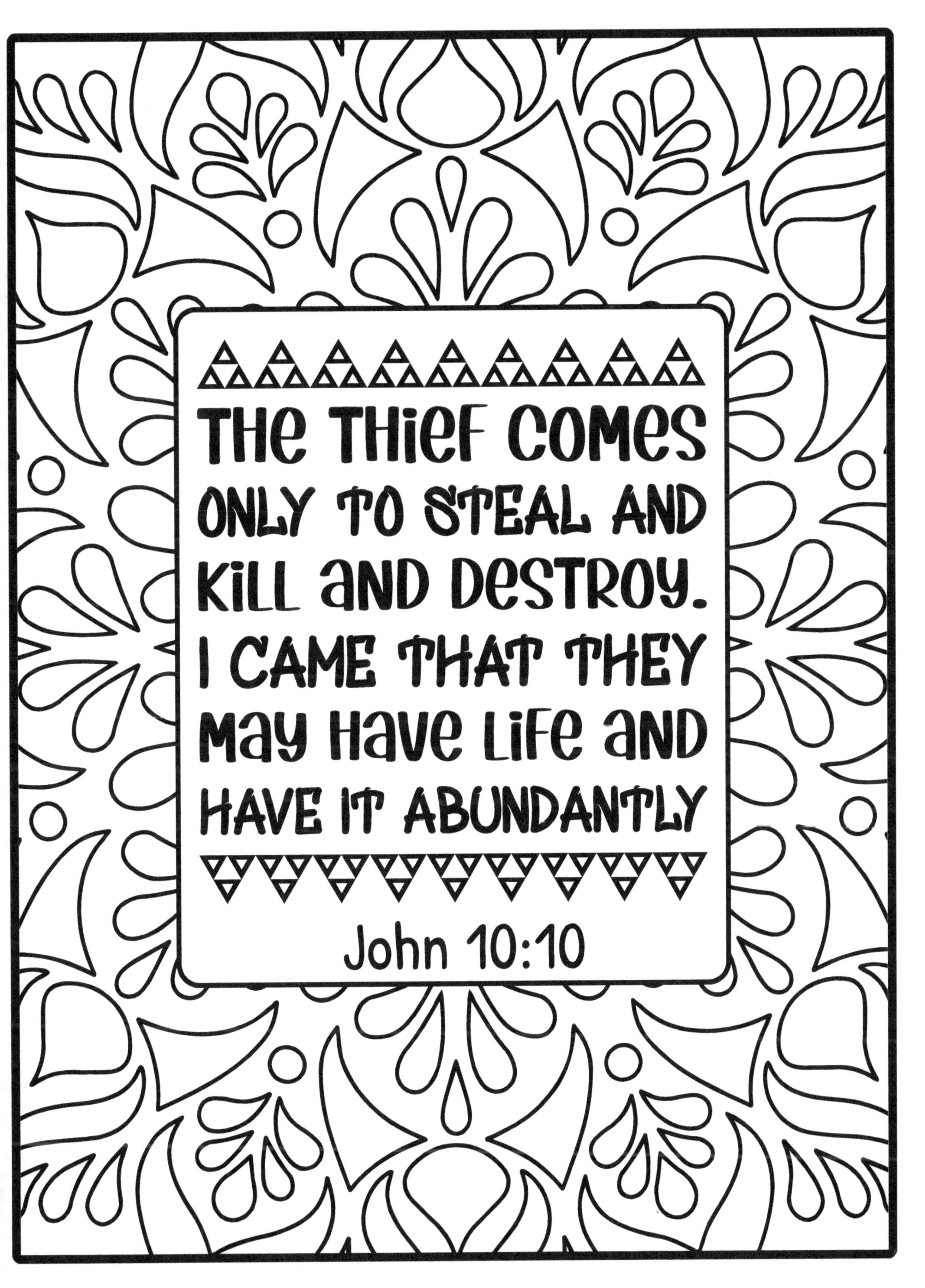

THE THIEF COMES ONLY TO STEAL AND KILL AND DESTROY. I CAME THAT THEY MAY HAVE LIFE AND HAVE IT ABUNDANTLY
John 10:10

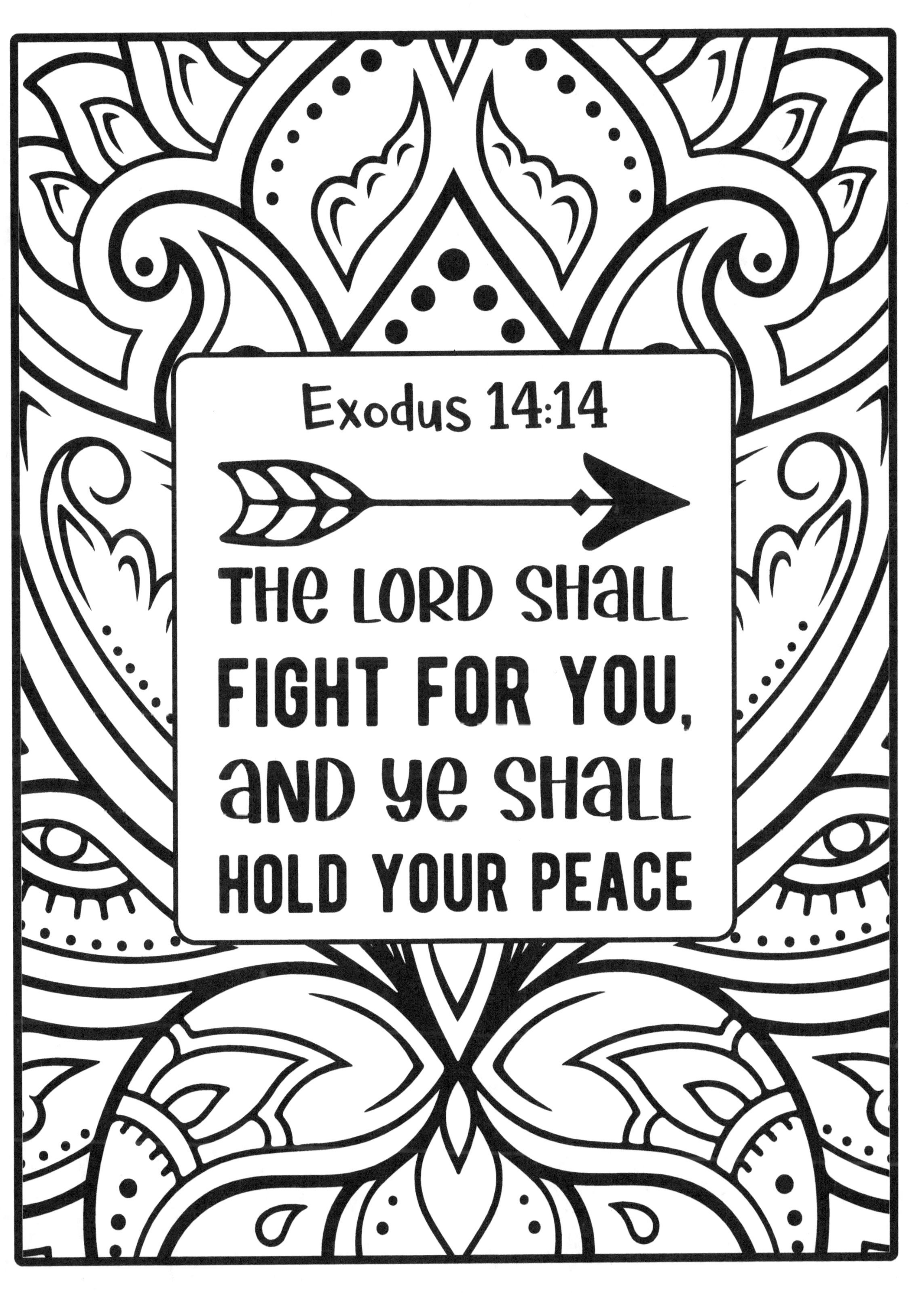

Exodus 14:14
THE LORD SHALL FIGHT FOR YOU, AND YE SHALL HOLD YOUR PEACE

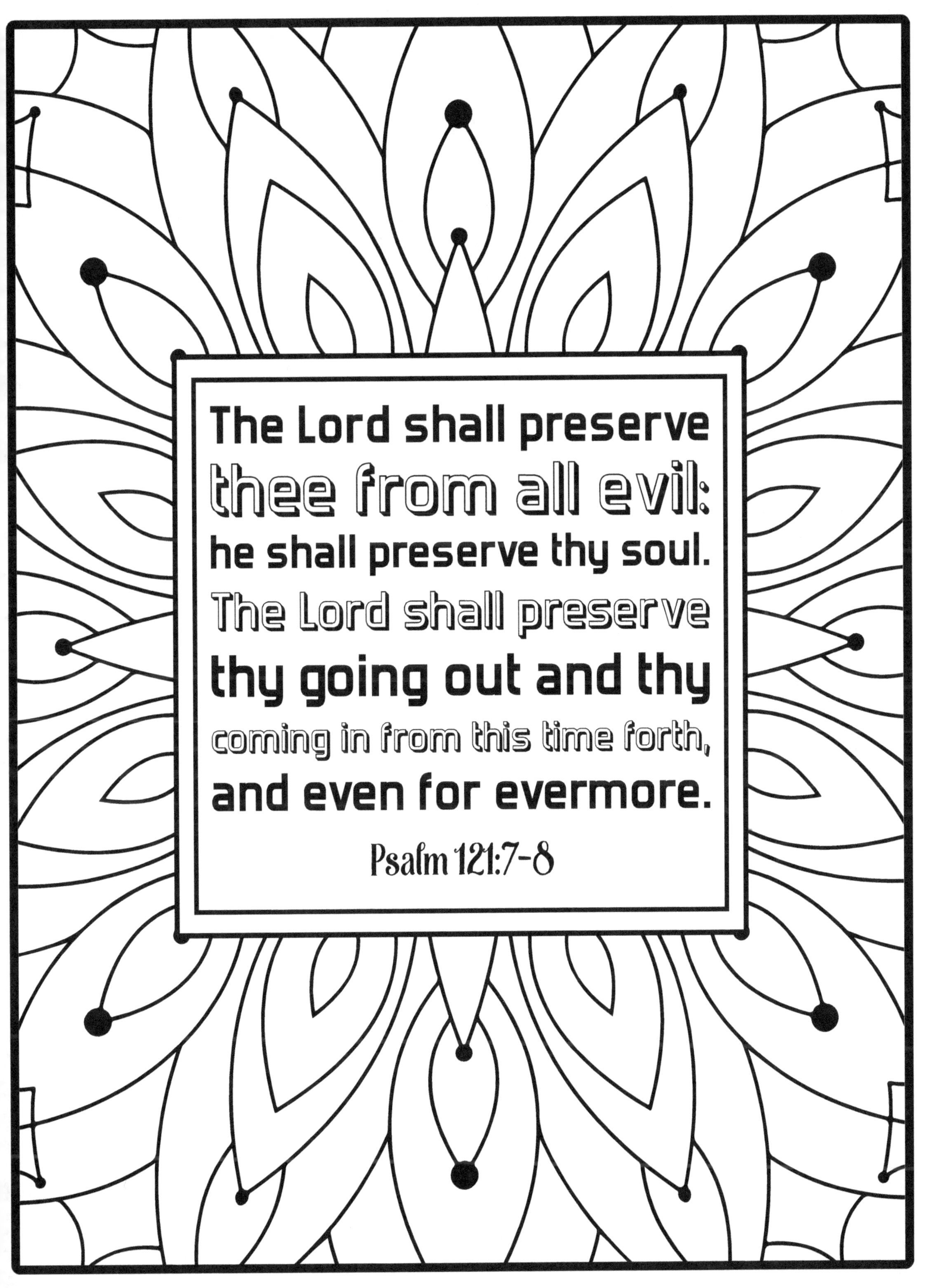

The Lord shall preserve thee from all evil: he shall preserve thy soul. The Lord shall preserve thy going out and thy coming in from this time forth, and even for evermore.
Psalm 121:7-8

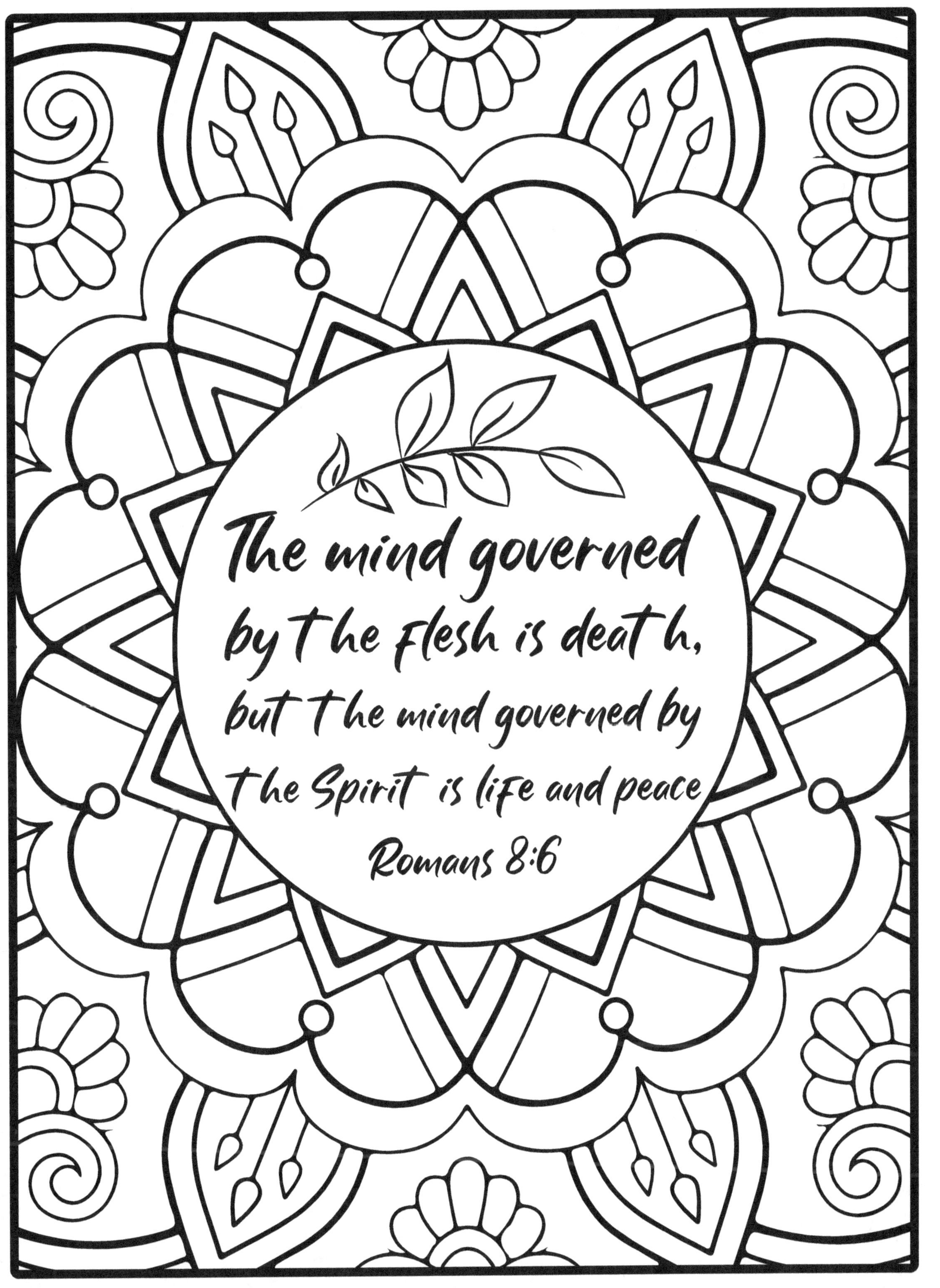

The mind governed
by the flesh is death,
but the mind governed by
the Spirit is life and peace
Romans 8:6

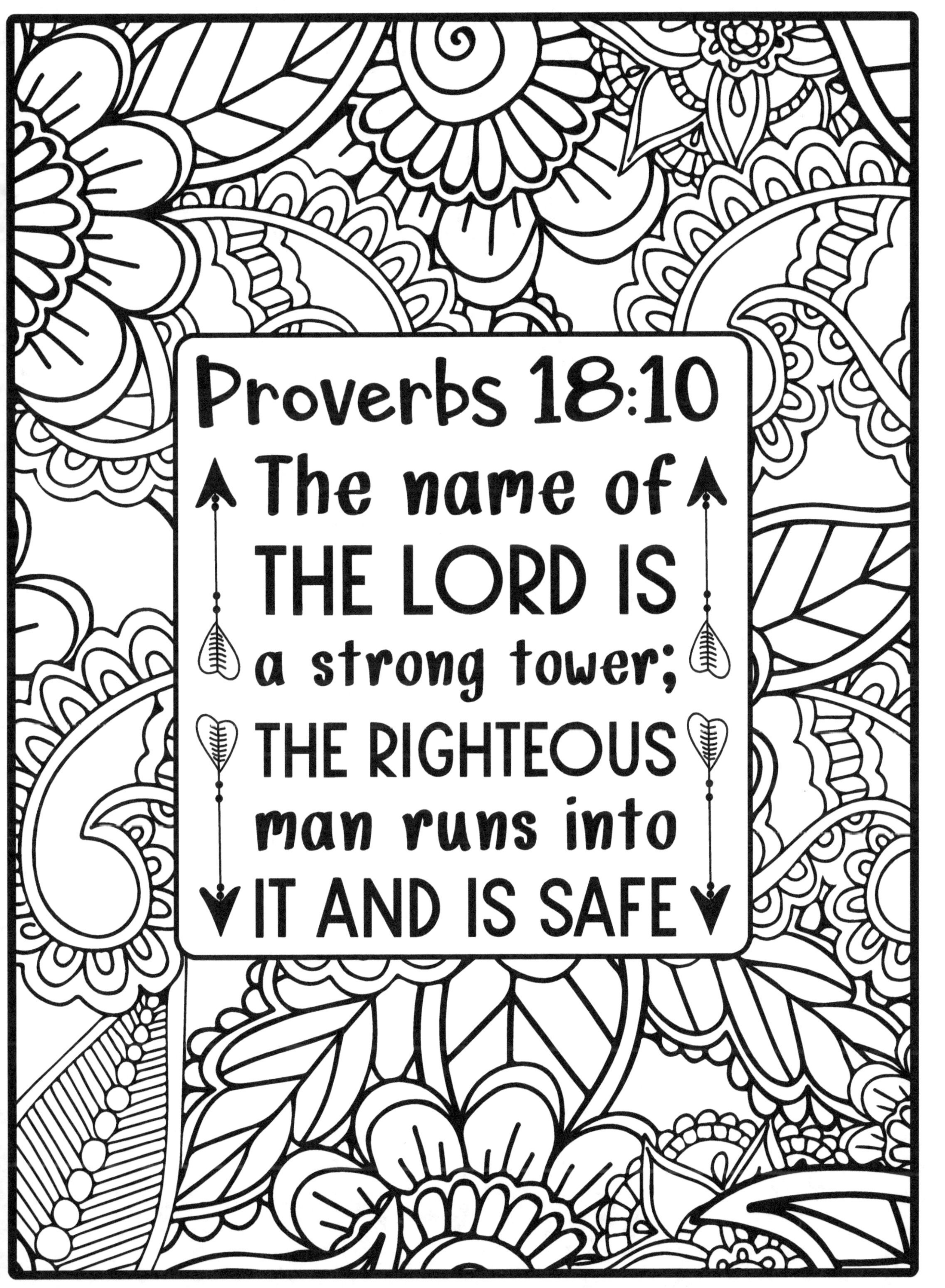

Proverbs 18:10
The name of
THE LORD IS
a strong tower;
THE RIGHTEOUS
man runs into
IT AND IS SAFE

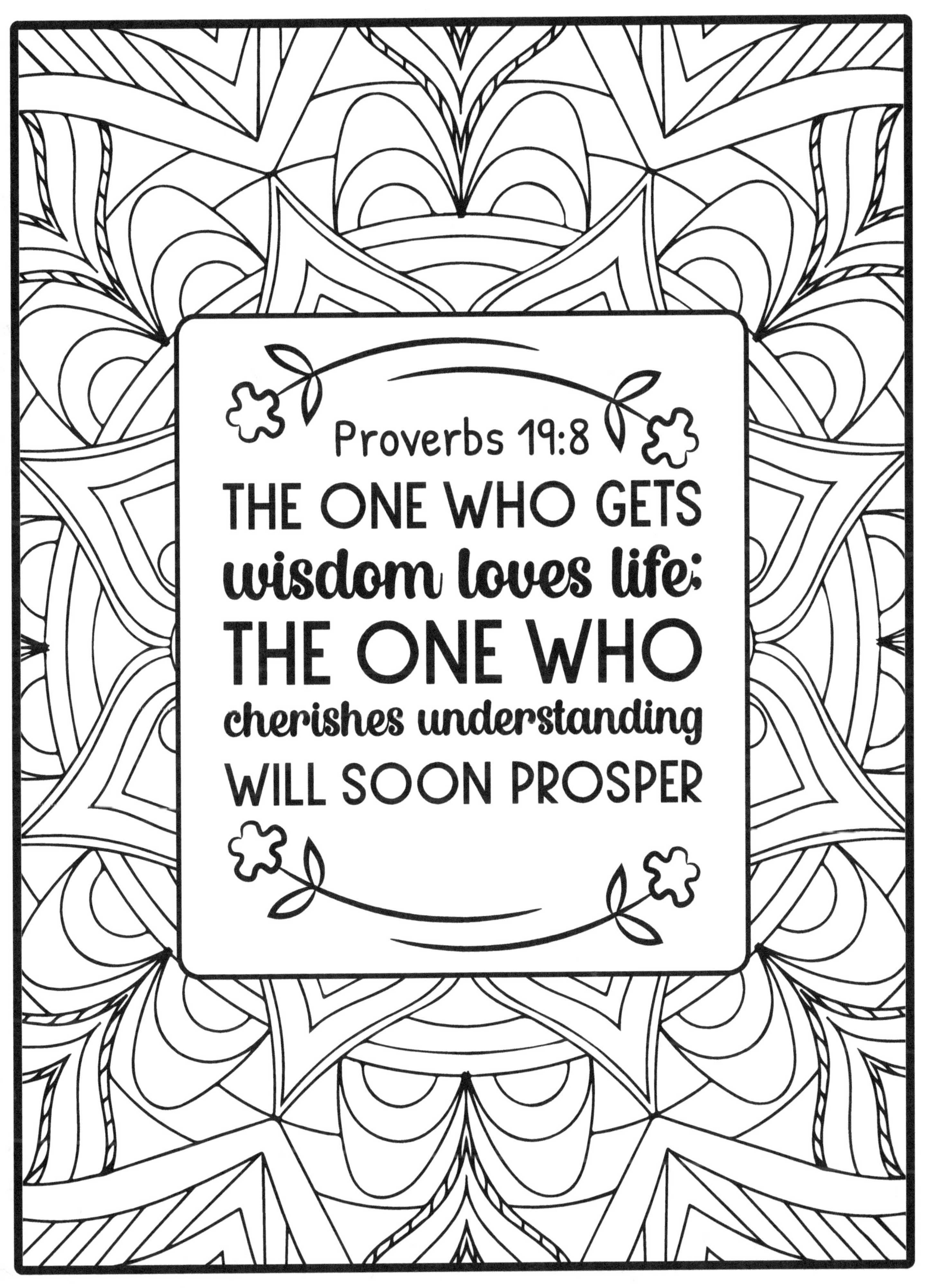
Proverbs 19:8
THE ONE WHO GETS
wisdom loves life;
THE ONE WHO
cherishes understanding
WILL SOON PROSPER

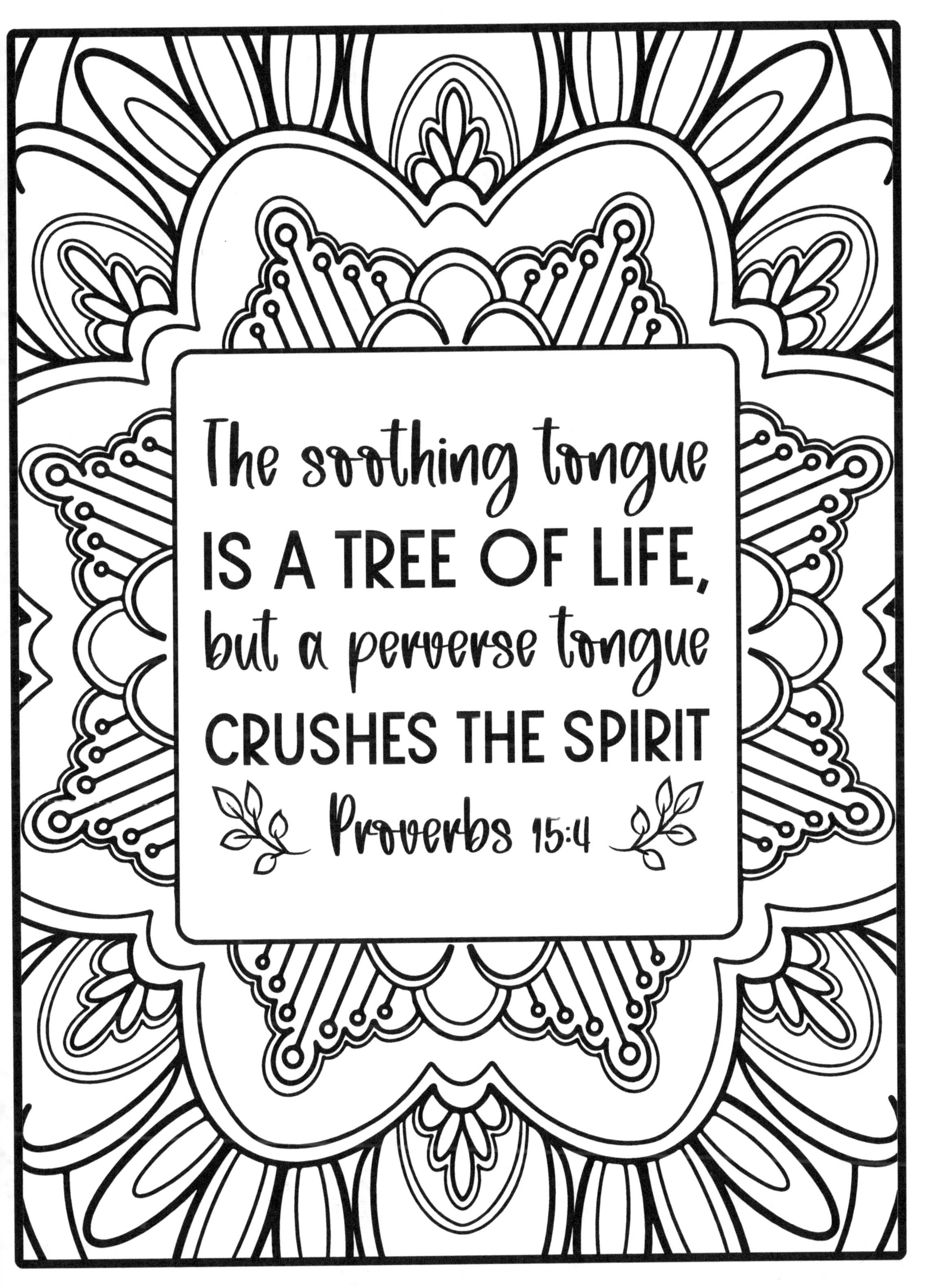

The soothing tongue
IS A TREE OF LIFE,
but a perverse tongue
CRUSHES THE SPIRIT
Proverbs 15:4

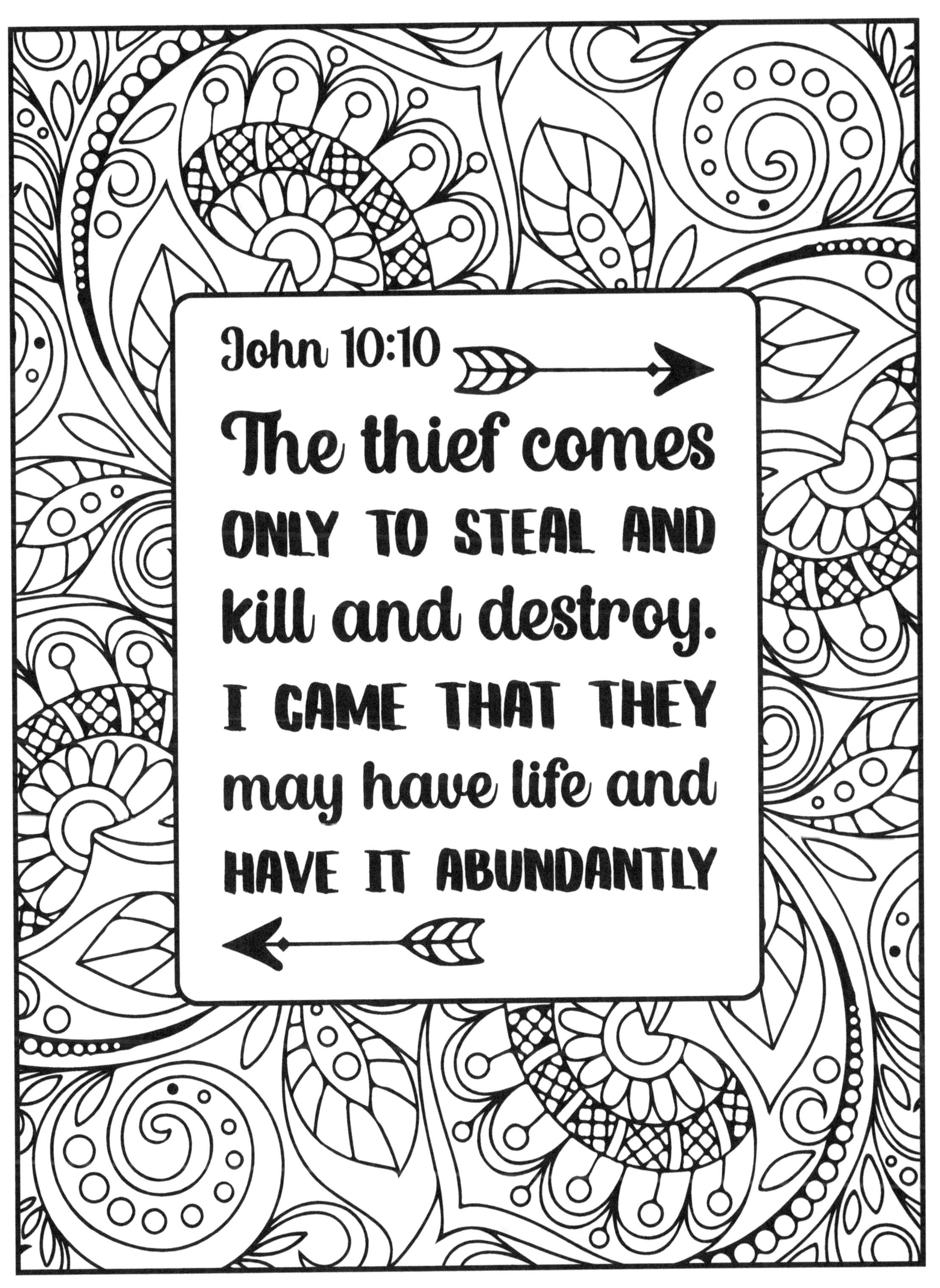

John 10:10
The thief comes only to steal and kill and destroy. I came that they may have life and have it abundantly

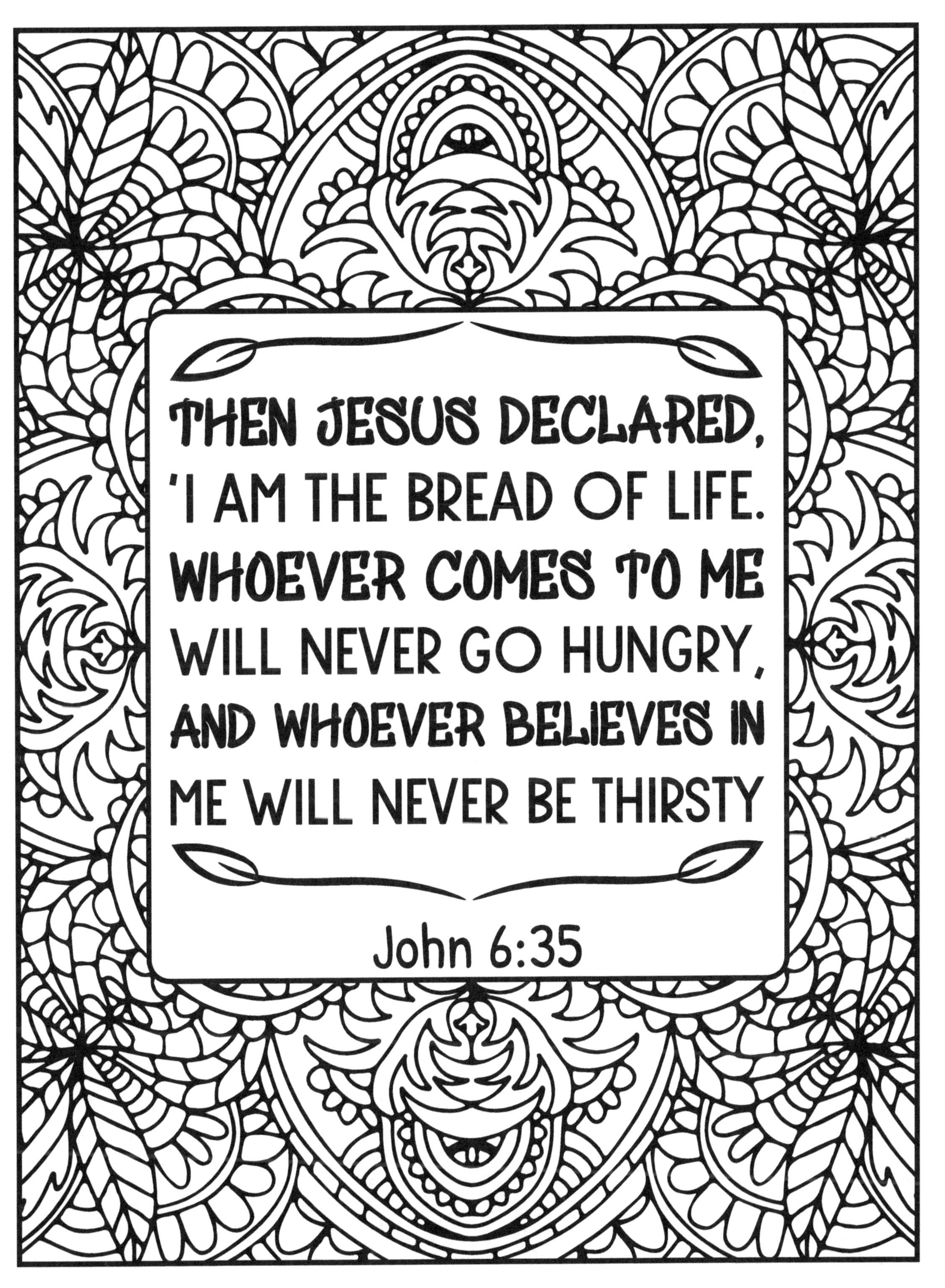

THEN JESUS DECLARED, 'I AM THE BREAD OF LIFE. WHOEVER COMES TO ME WILL NEVER GO HUNGRY, AND WHOEVER BELIEVES IN ME WILL NEVER BE THIRSTY
John 6:35

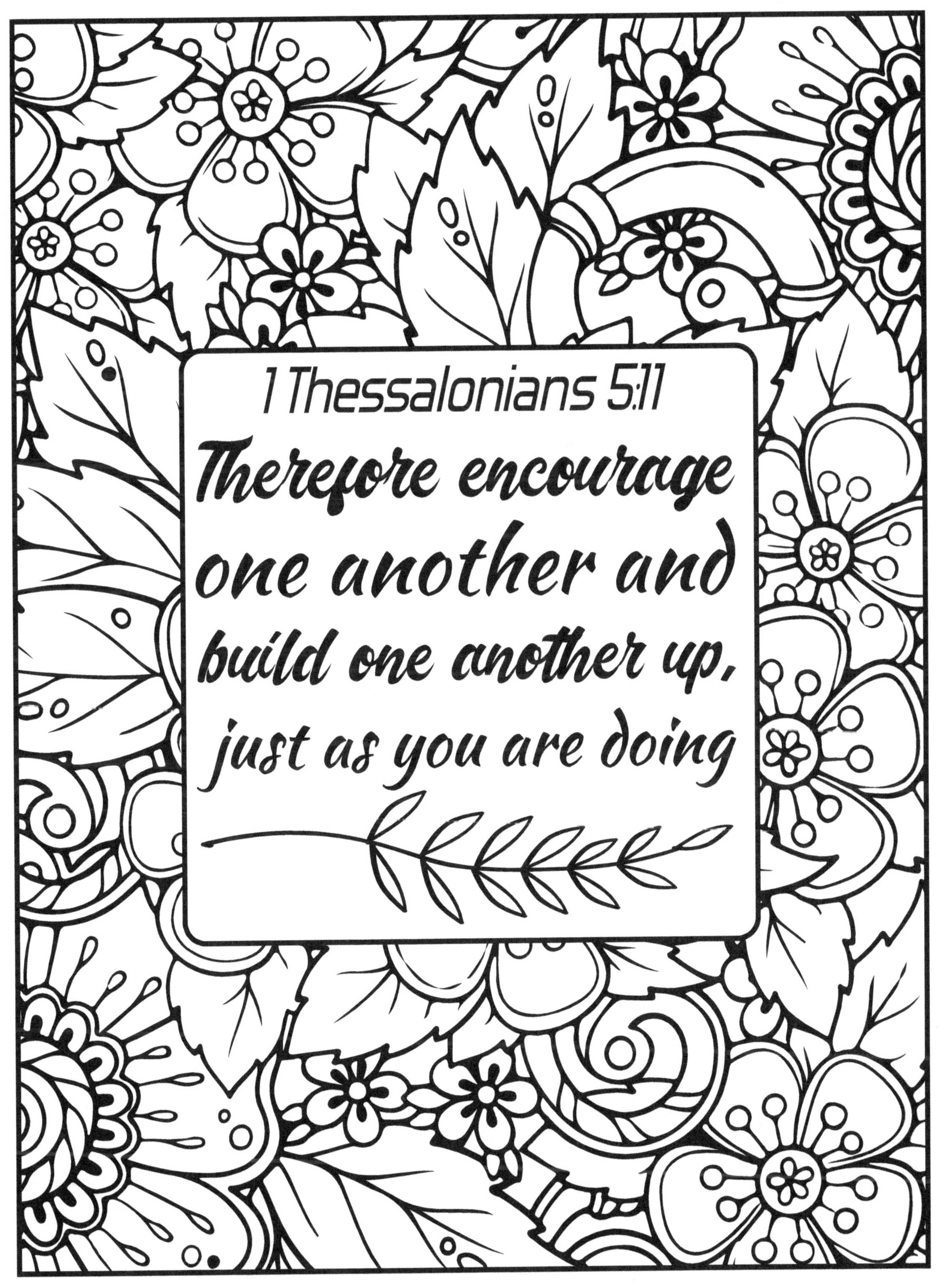

1 Thessalonians 5:11
Therefore encourage one another and build one another up, just as you are doing

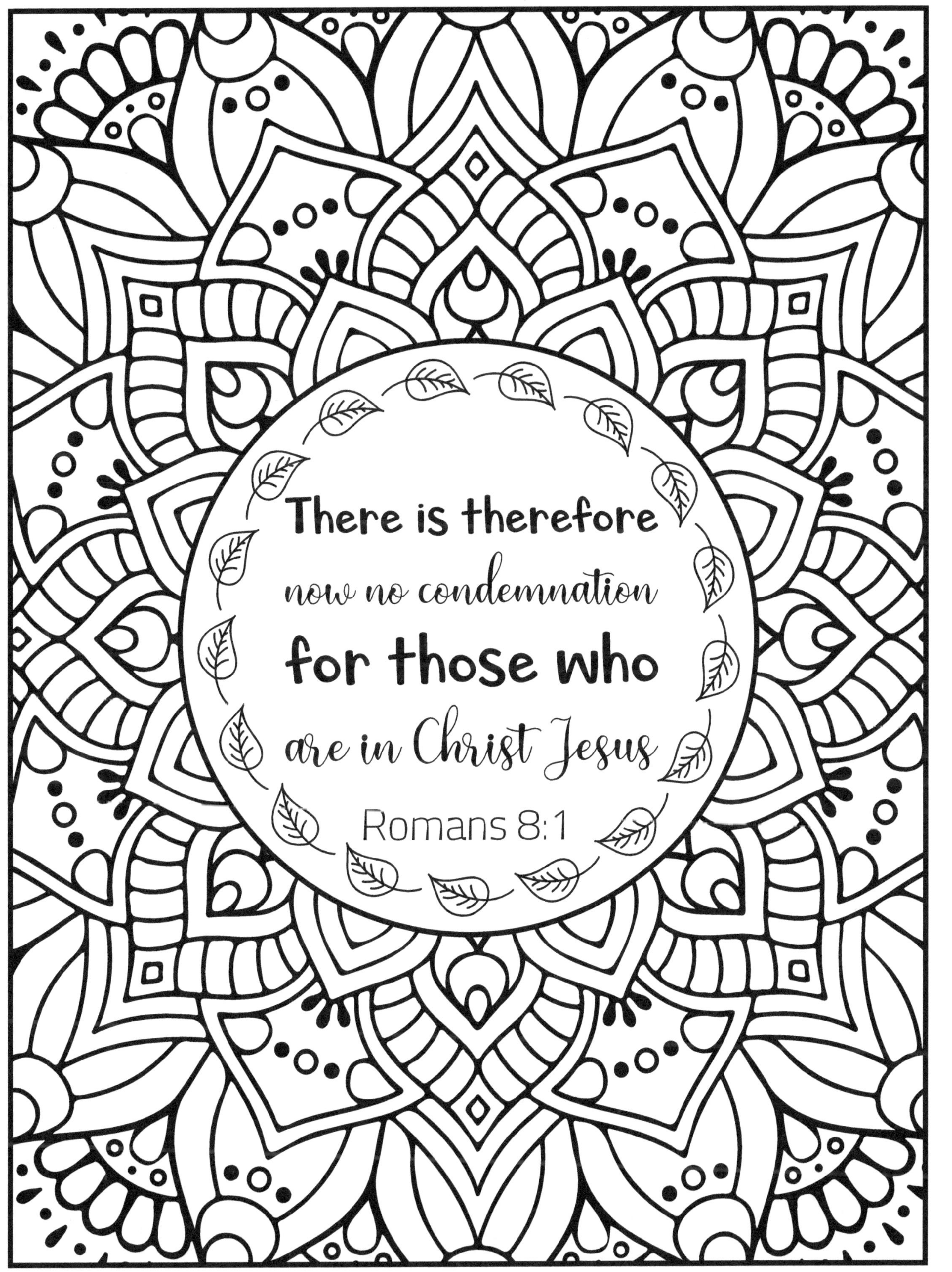

There is therefore
now no condemnation
for those who
are in Christ Jesus
Romans 8:1

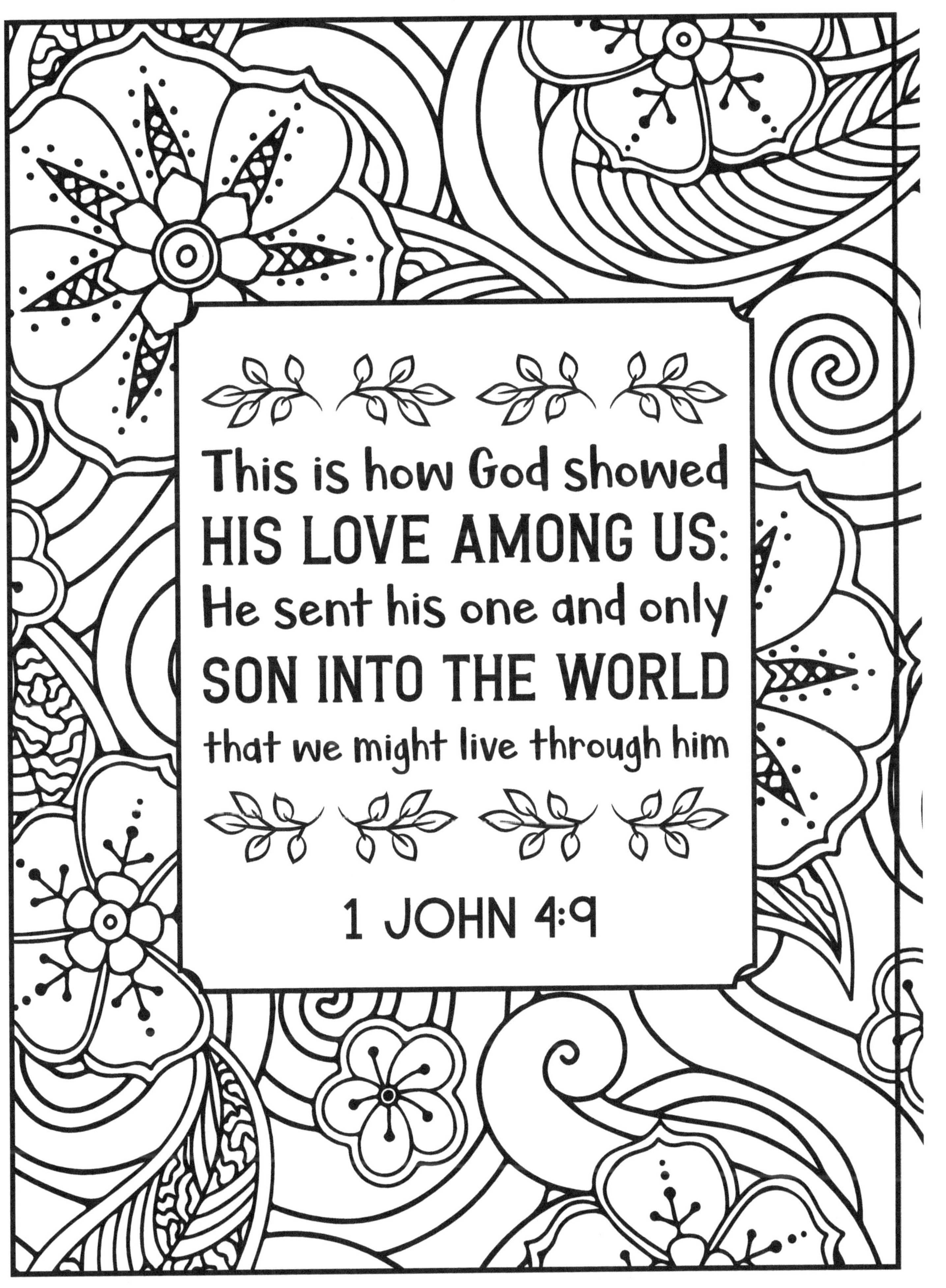

This is how God showed
HIS LOVE AMONG US:
He sent his one and only
SON INTO THE WORLD
that we might live through him

1 JOHN 4:9

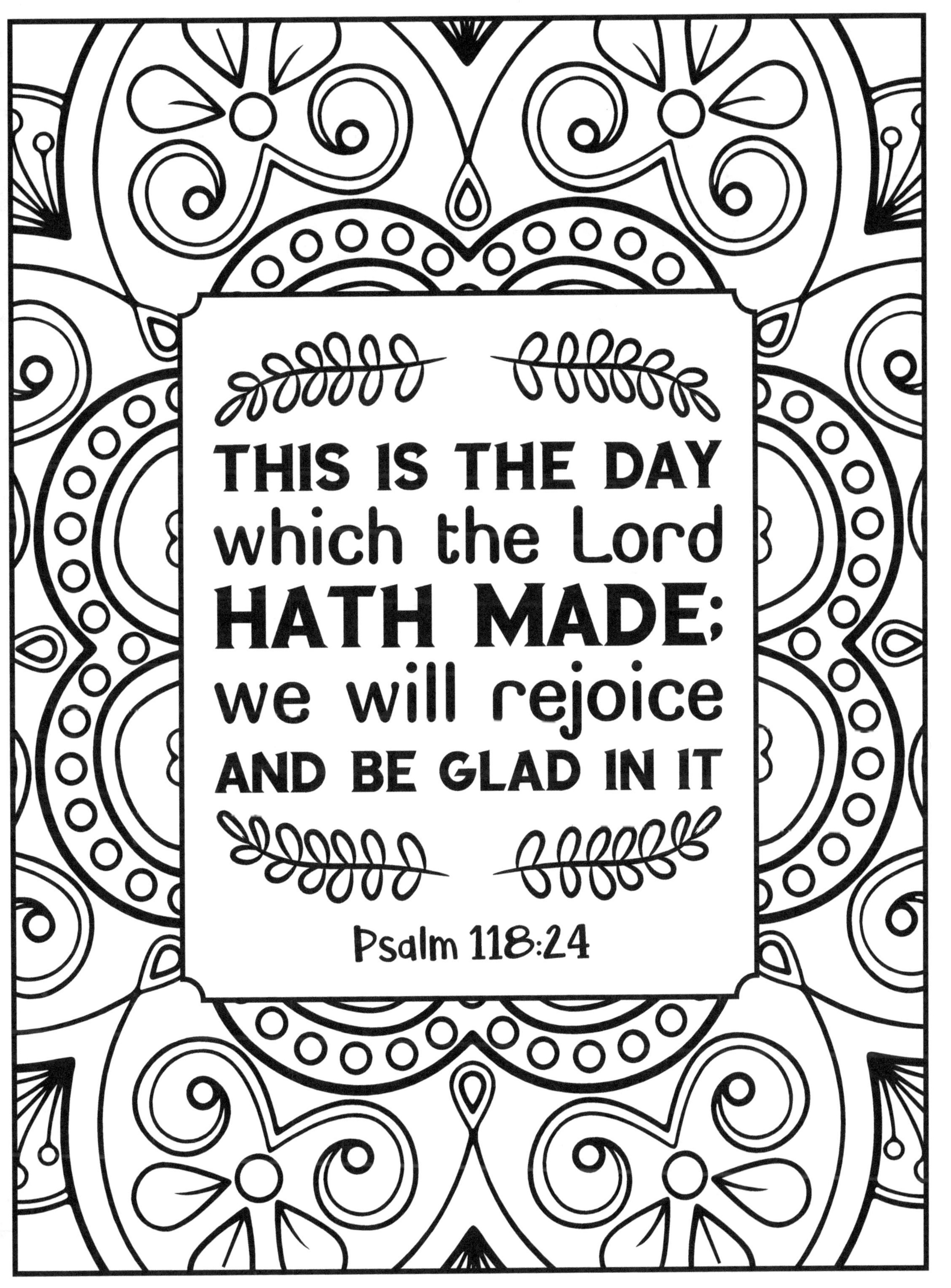

THIS IS THE DAY
which the Lord
HATH MADE;
we will rejoice
AND BE GLAD IN IT
Psalm 118:24

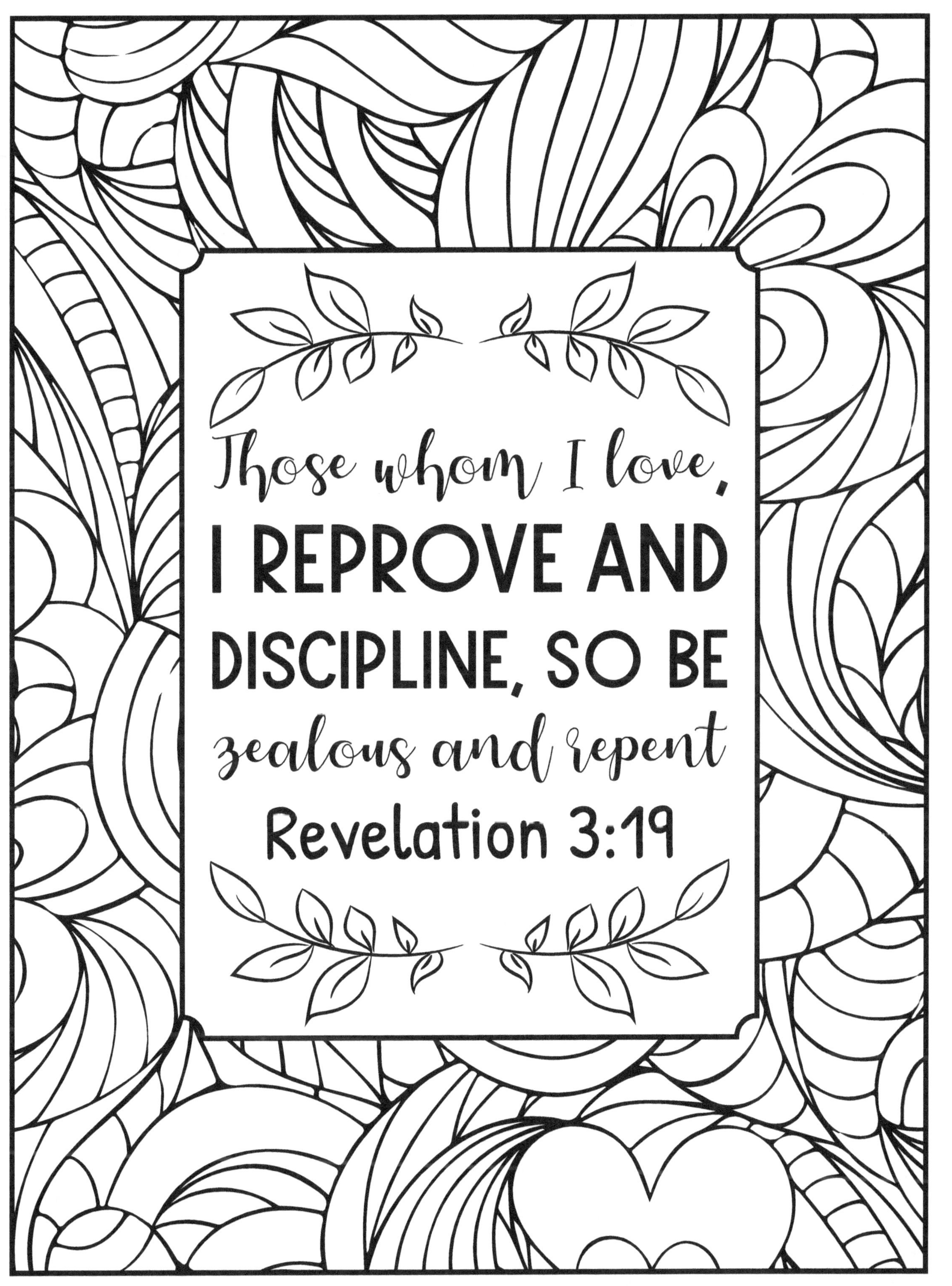

Those whom I love,
I REPROVE AND
DISCIPLINE, SO BE
zealous and repent
Revelation 3:19

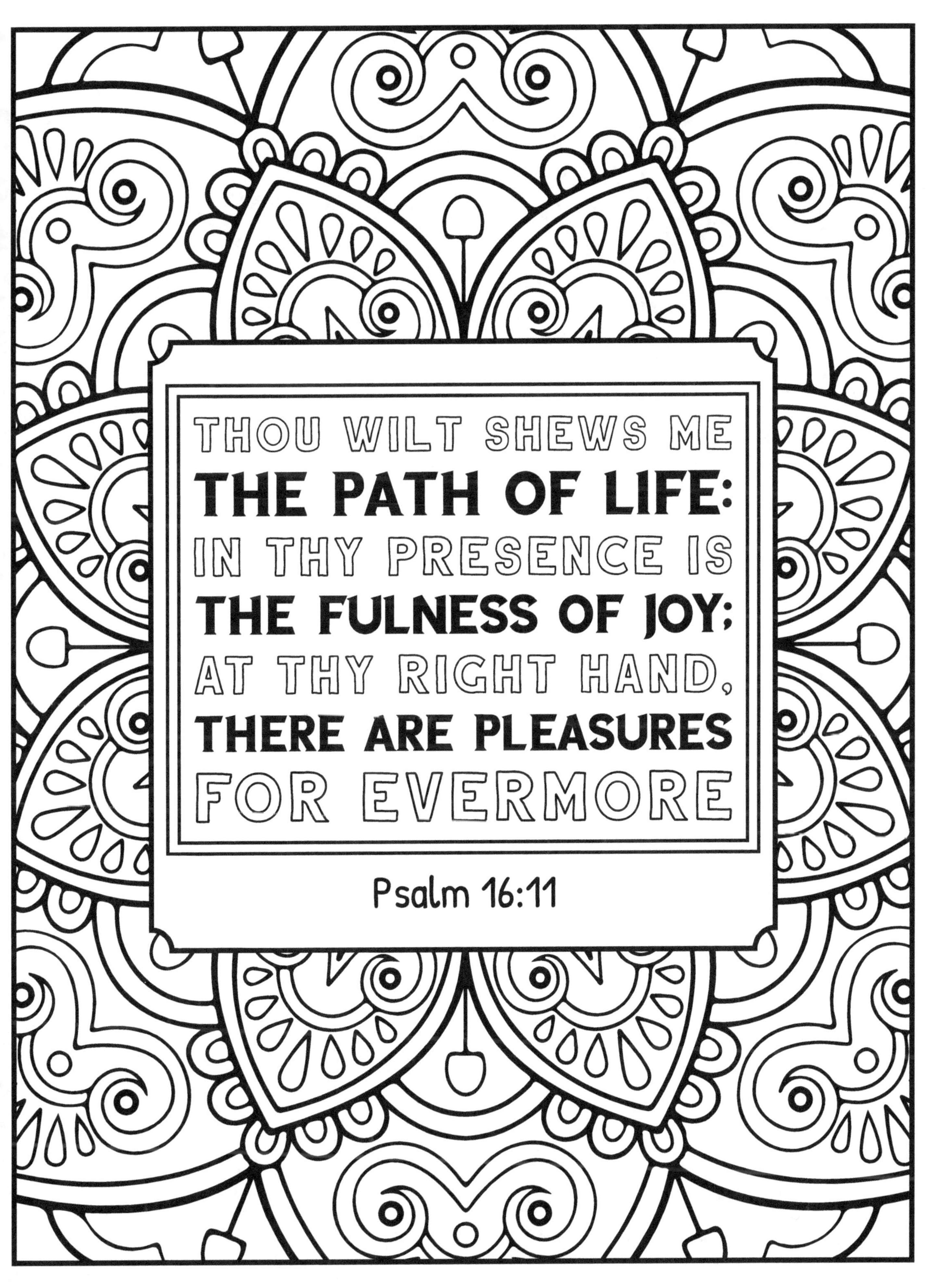

THOU WILT SHEWS ME
THE PATH OF LIFE:
IN THY PRESENCE IS
THE FULNESS OF JOY;
AT THY RIGHT HAND,
THERE ARE PLEASURES
FOR EVERMORE
Psalm 16:11

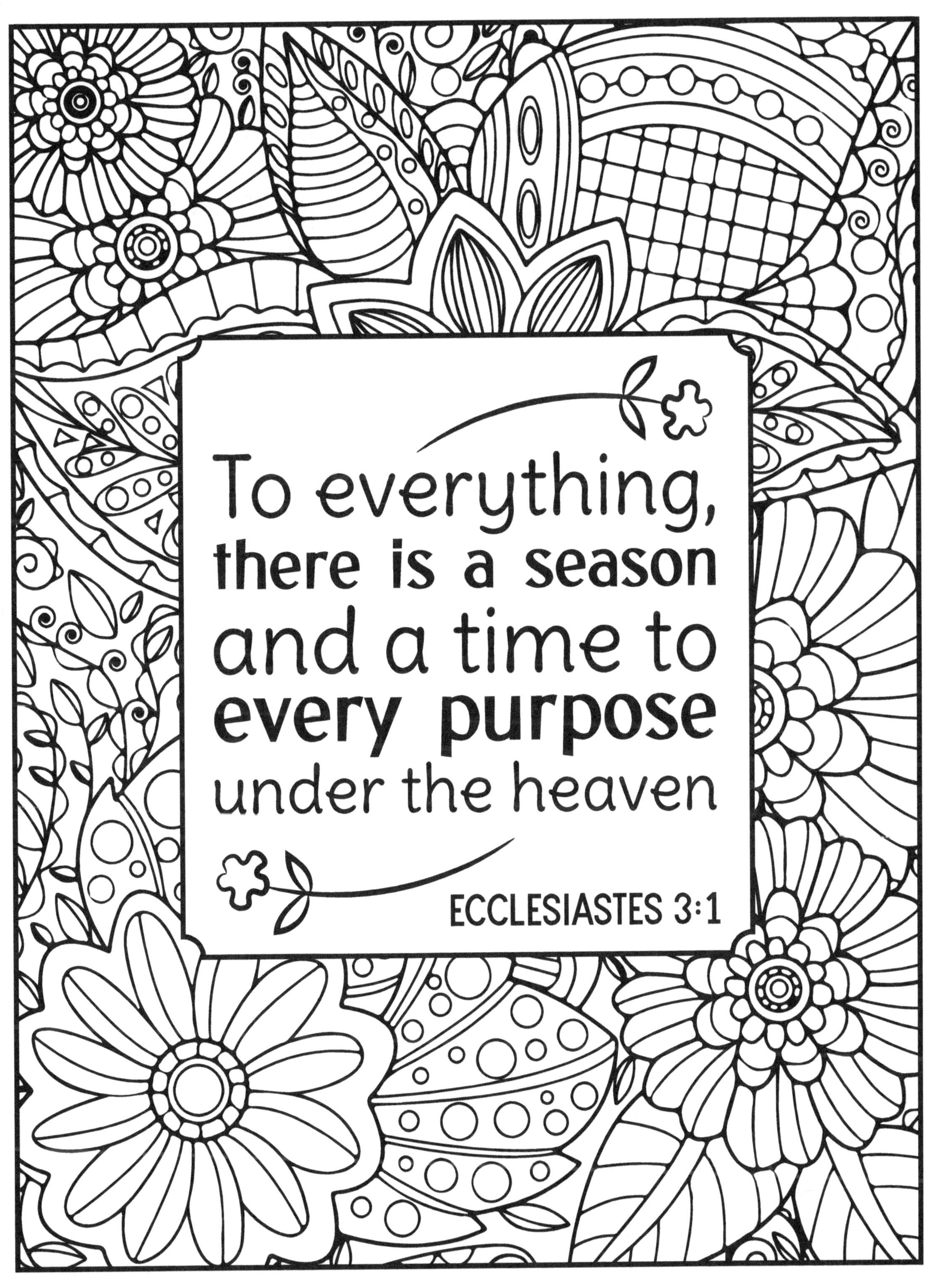

To everything,
there is a season
and a time to
every purpose
under the heaven

ECCLESIASTES 3:1

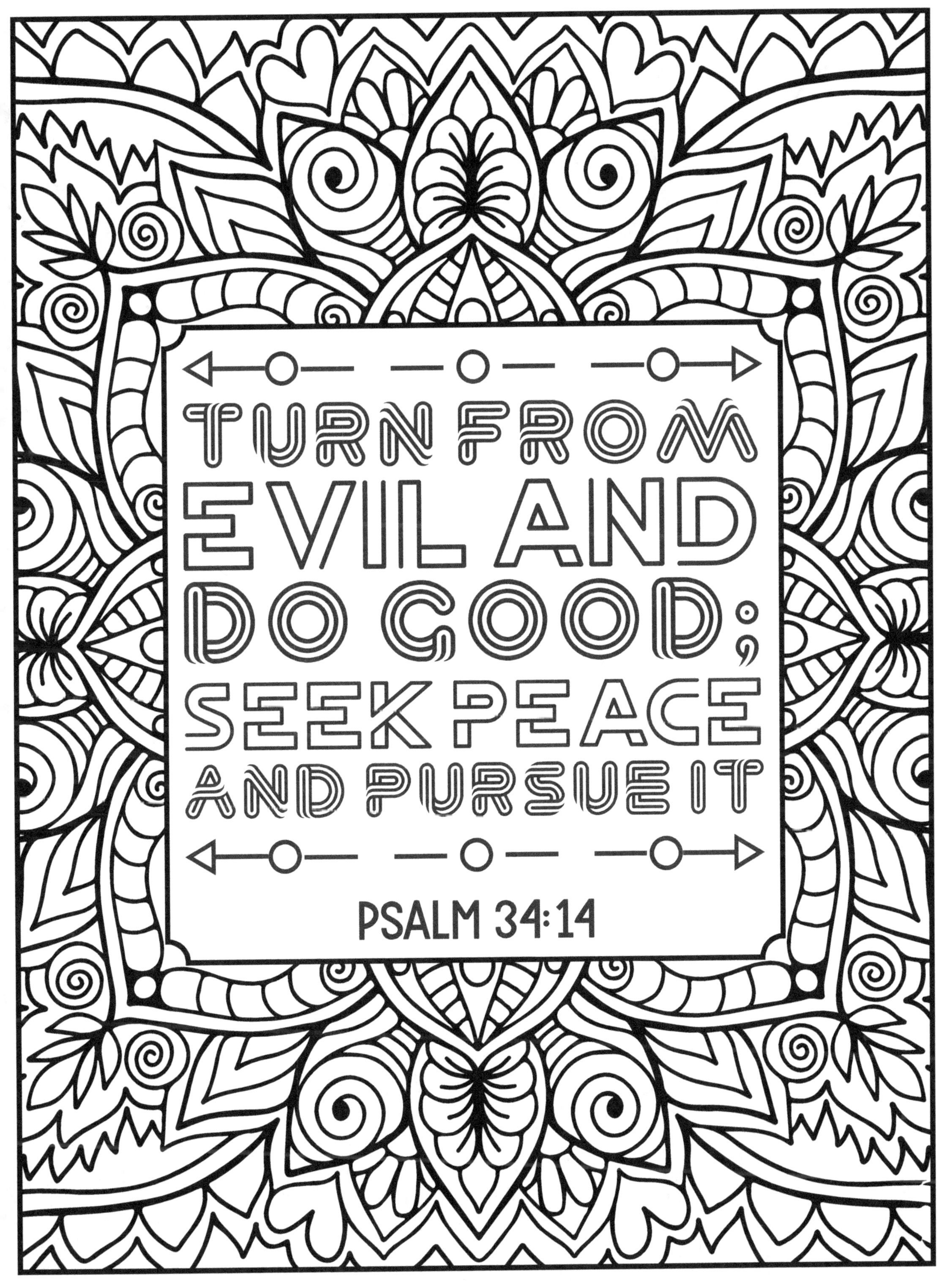

TURN FROM
EVIL AND
DO GOOD;
SEEK PEACE
AND PURSUE IT
PSALM 34:14

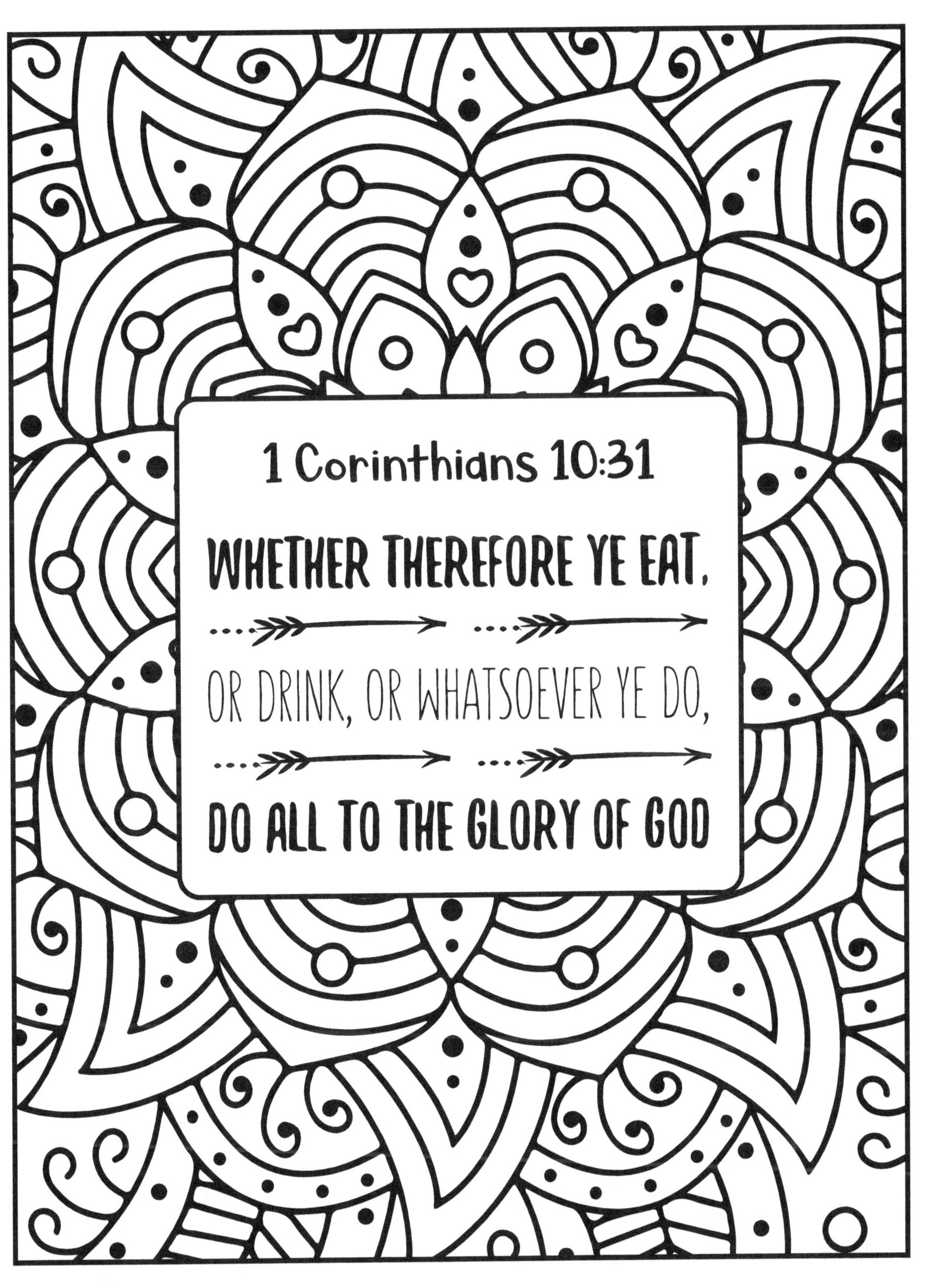

1 Corinthians 10:31

WHETHER THEREFORE YE EAT,

OR DRINK, OR WHATSOEVER YE DO,

DO ALL TO THE GLORY OF GOD

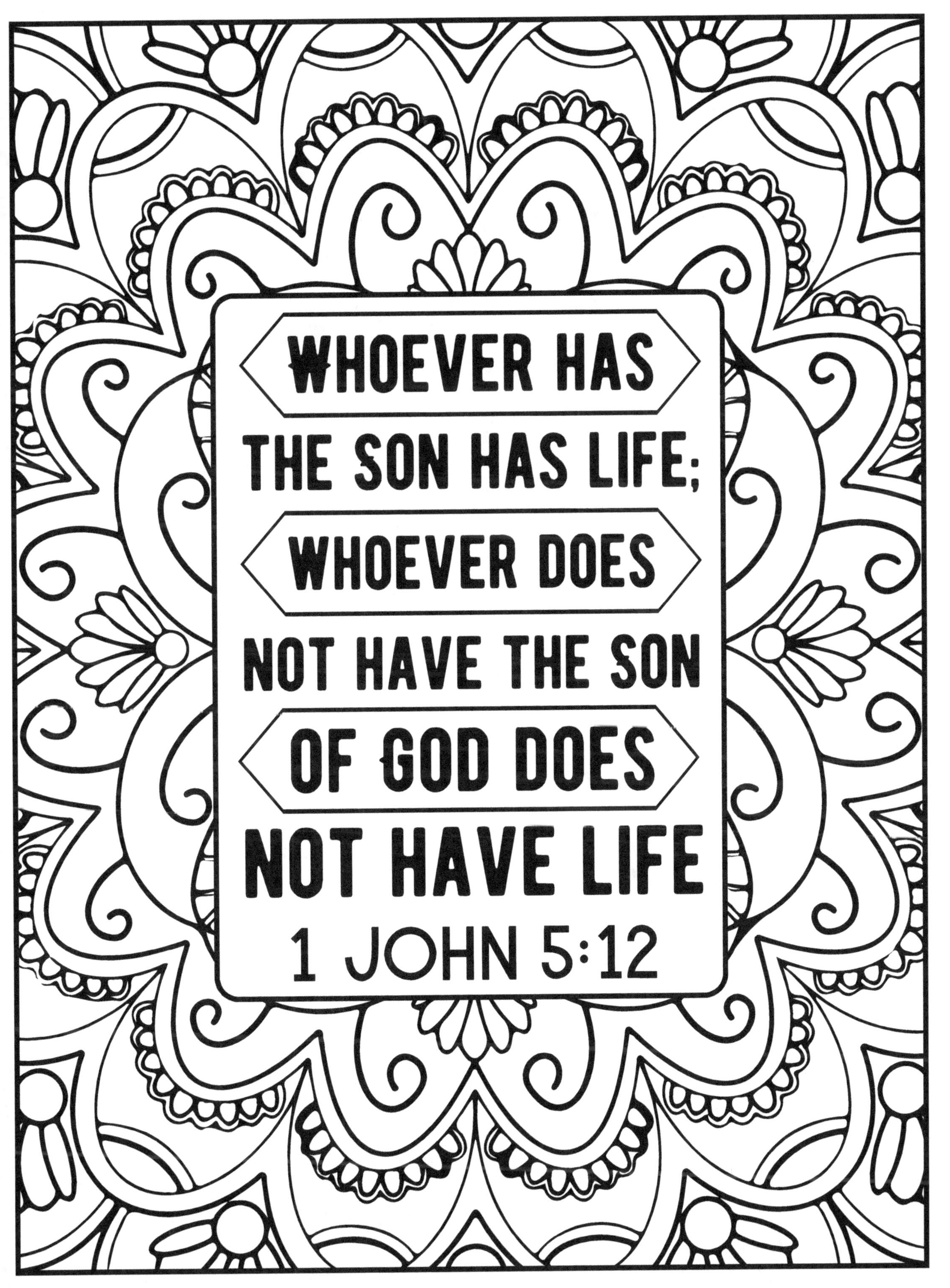

WHOEVER HAS
THE SON HAS LIFE;
WHOEVER DOES
NOT HAVE THE SON
OF GOD DOES
NOT HAVE LIFE
1 JOHN 5:12

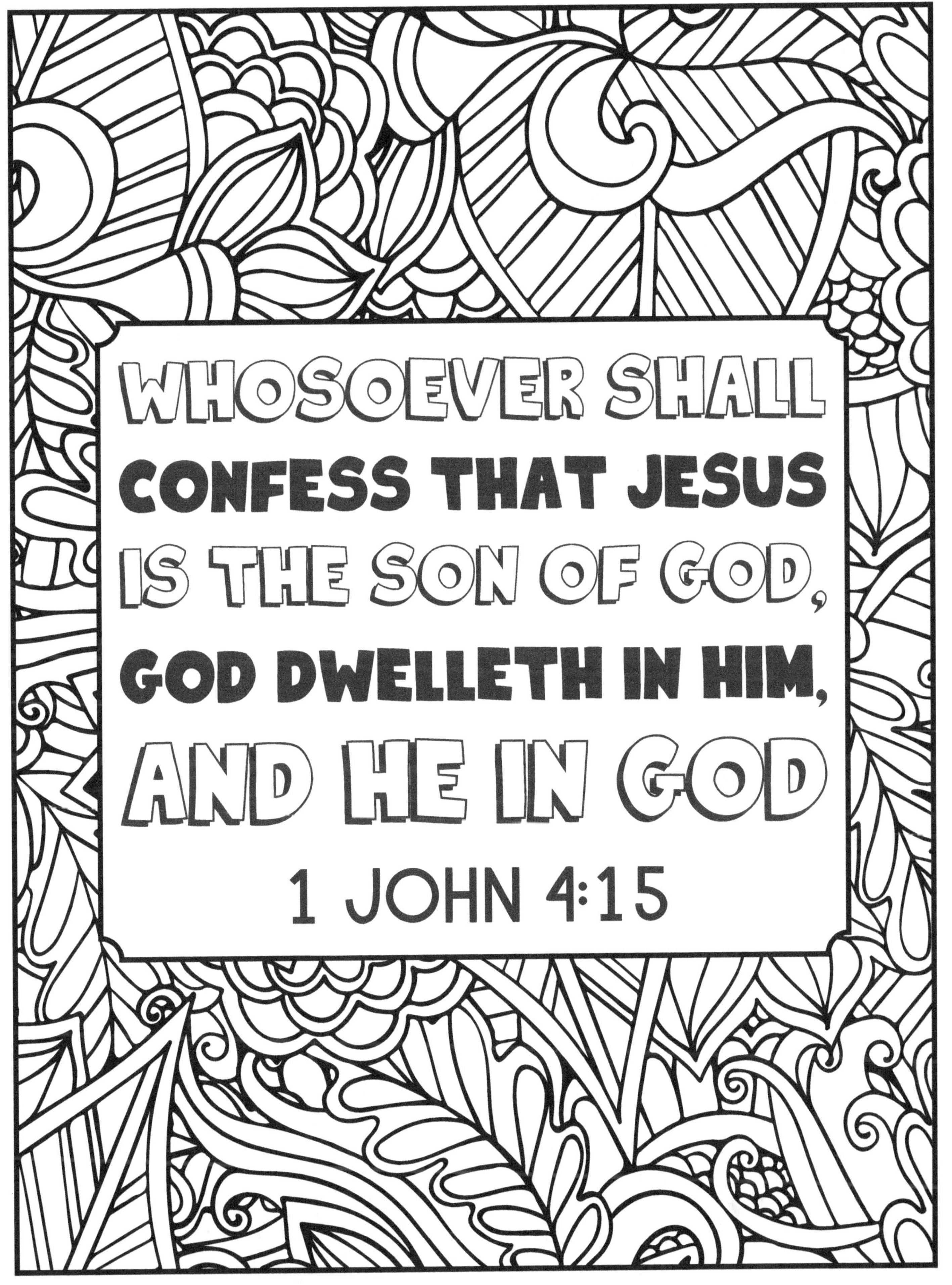

WHOSOEVER SHALL CONFESS THAT JESUS IS THE SON OF GOD, GOD DWELLETH IN HIM, AND HE IN GOD
1 JOHN 4:15

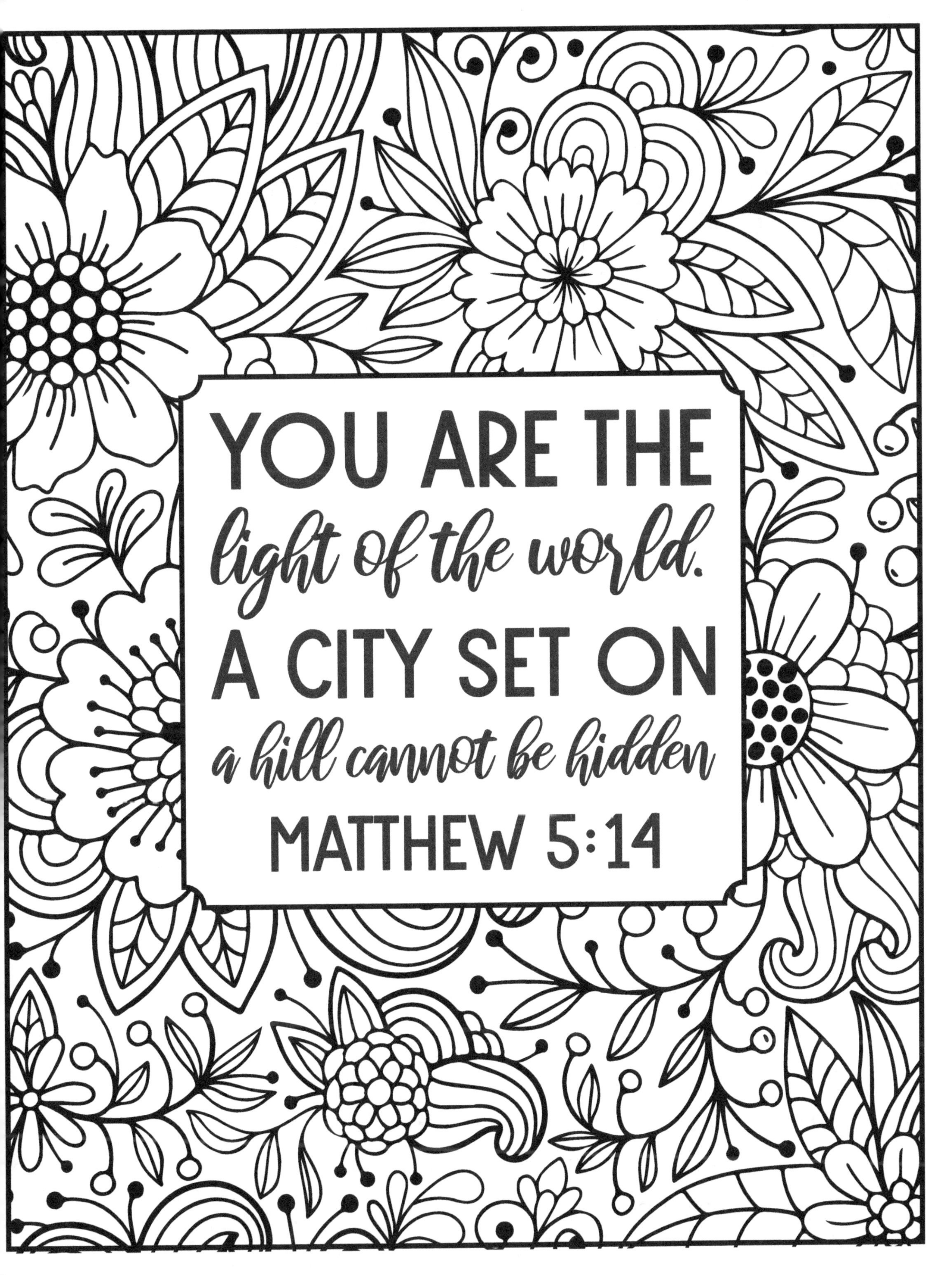

YOU ARE THE
light of the world.
A CITY SET ON
a hill cannot be hidden
MATTHEW 5:14

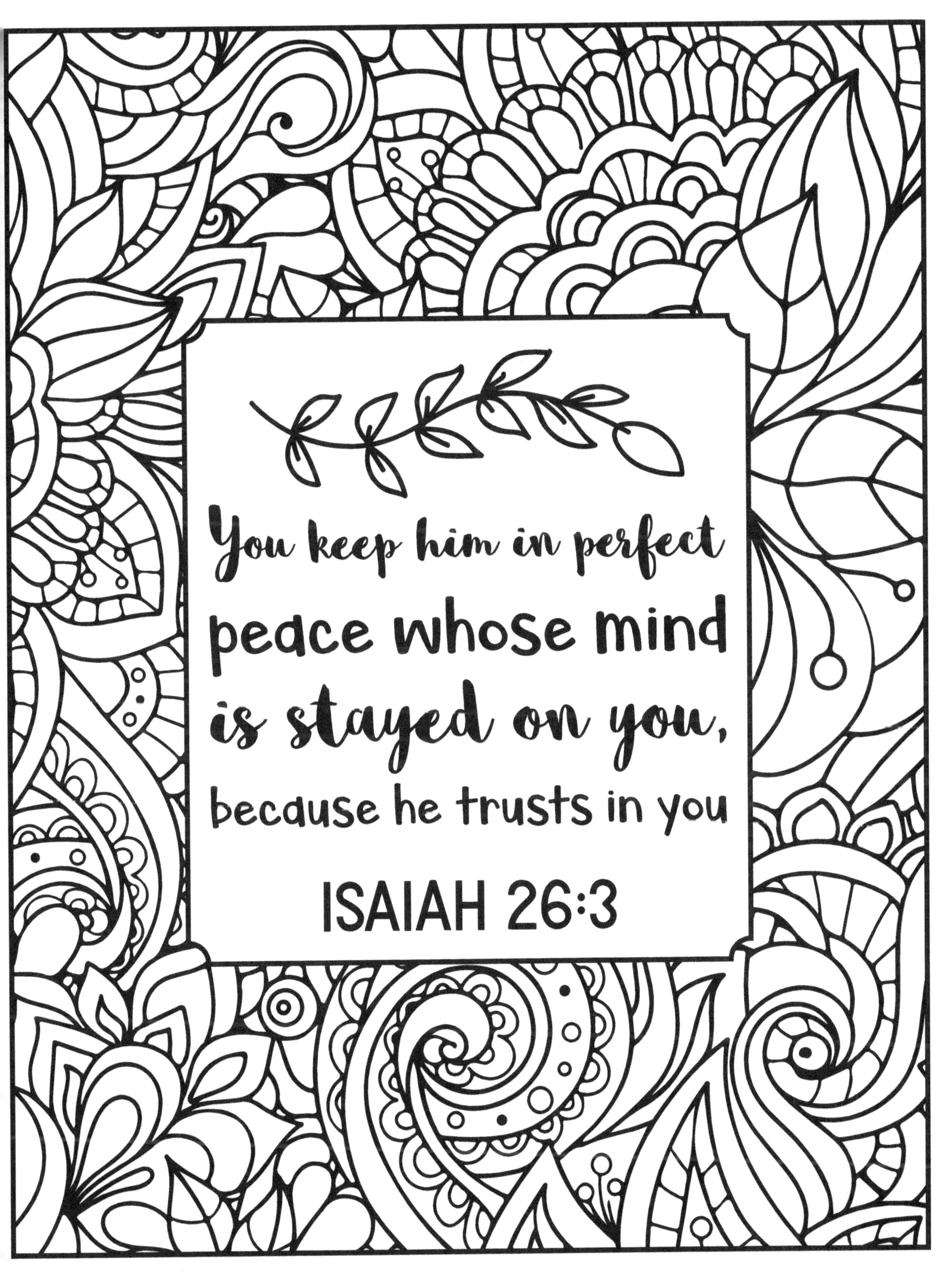

You keep him in perfect peace whose mind is stayed on you, because he trusts in you
ISAIAH 26:3

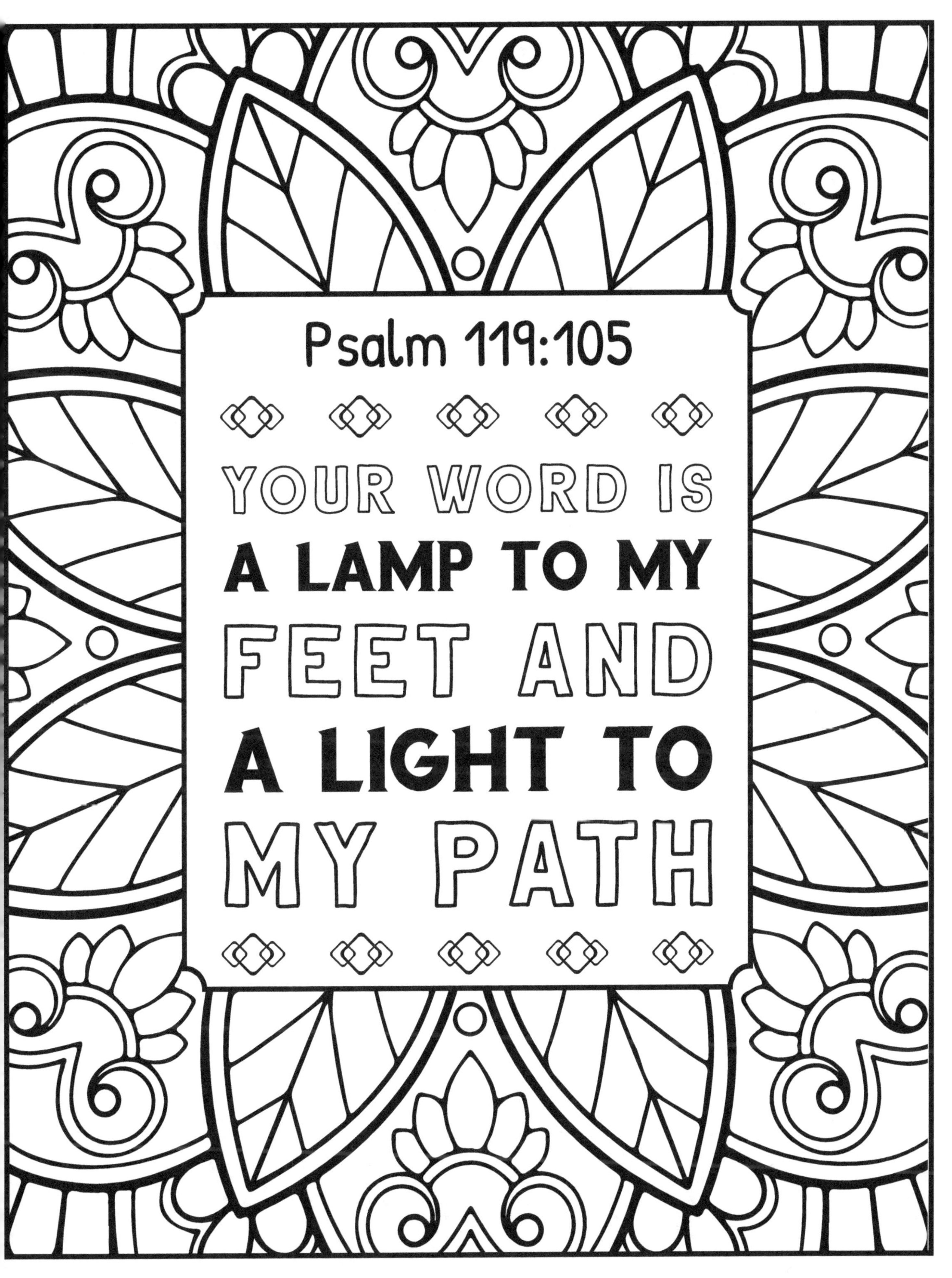
Psalm 119:105
YOUR WORD IS
A LAMP TO MY
FEET AND
A LIGHT TO
MY PATH

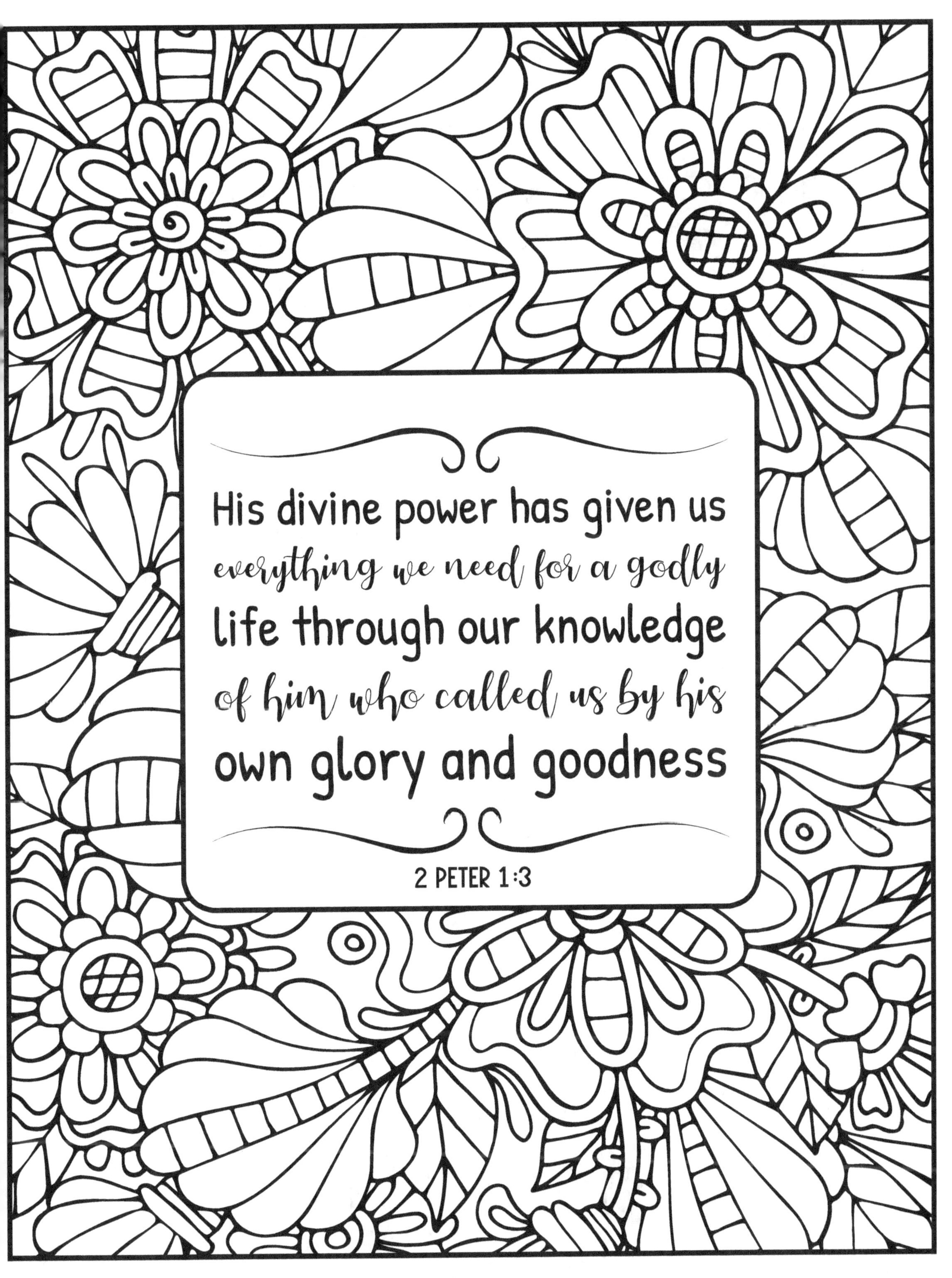

His divine power has given us everything we need for a godly life through our knowledge of him who called us by his own glory and goodness
2 PETER 1:3

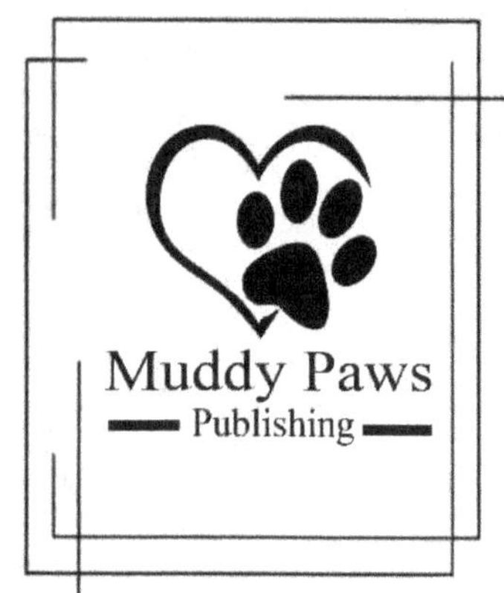

WE HAVE A **FREE** GIFT FOR YOU

Tell us where to send your free digital activity book
for kids

email muddypawspublishing@gmail.com

If your little one enjoyed this book

please consider leaving an honest review on Amazon.com

Thank you

SEARCH FOR MUDDY PAWS PUBLISHING
ON AMAZON FOR MORE FUN FOR YOUR LITTLE ONE

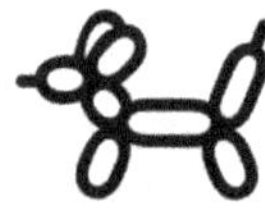

@muddypawspublishing

 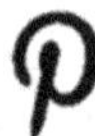 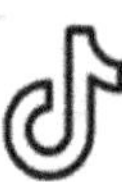 Etsy

www.ingramcontent.com/pod-product-compliance
Lightning Source LLC
Chambersburg PA
CBHW081927120726
47997CB00010B/3068